fast fresh. vegetarian

Published in 2013 by Bauer Media Books, Sydney
Bauer Media Books are published by Bauer Media Limited.

BAUER MEDIA GROUP

BAUER MEDIA BOOKS
Publishing director Gerry Reynolds
Publisher Sally Wright
Editorial & food director Pamela Clark
Director of sales, marketing & rights Brian Cearnes
Creative director Hieu Chi Nguyen
Art director & designer Hannah Blackmore
Senior editor Stephanie Kistner
Food concept director Sophia Young
Food editor Alexandra Elliott
Marketing manager Bridget Cody
Senior business analyst Rebecca Varela
Operations manager David Scotto
Production controller Corinne Whitsun-Jones

Published by Bauer Media Books,
a division of Bauer Media Ltd,
54 Park St, Sydney; GPO Box 4088, Sydney, NSW 2001.
phone (02) 9282 8618; fax (02) 9267 9438
www.awwcookbooks.com.au

Photographer William Meppem
Stylist Vivien Walsh
Photochef Adam Cremona

Recipe developers Olivia Andrews,
Adam Cremona, Alexandra Elliott,
Lucy Nunes, Elizabeth Macri,
Alexandra Somerville, Sophia Young

The publisher would like to
thank Murobond for props
used in photography.

Printed in China with 1010 Printing Asia Limited.

Australia Distributed by Network Services,
phone +61 2 9282 8777; fax +61 2 9264 3278;
networkweb@networkservicescompany.com.au
New Zealand Distributed by Southern Publishers Group,
phone +64 9 419 2635; fax +64 9 419 2634
hub@spg.co.nz
South Africa Distributed by PSD Promotions,
phone +27 11 392 6065/6/7; fax +27 11 392 6079/80;
orders@psdprom.co.za

Title: Fast fresh vegetarian.
ISBN: 978-1-74245-302-6 (paperback with flaps.)
Notes: Includes index.
Subjects: Vegetarian cookery.
Other Authors/Contributors: Clark, Pamela.
Also Titled: Australian women's weekly.
Dewey Number: 641.5636

To order books
phone 136 116 (within Australia) or
order online at www.awwcookbooks.com.au
Send recipe enquiries to:
recipeenquiries@bauer-media.com.au

THE AUSTRALIAN Women's Weekly

fast fresh. vegetarian

contents

introduction 6

vegetables 8

pulses & grains 10

special ingredients 12

soups 14

salads 44

vegetables 70

cheese & eggs 94

grains & pulses 112

pasta & couscous 136

curries 162

weekend specials 178

glossary 234

conversion chart 237

index 238

introduction

This cookbook will change your perception of vegetarian food. In the past it has had a reputation of being bland, boring and unappetising. Well, no more. This selection of contemporary and delicious meat-free recipes will show you just how much has changed.

As a society, we're becoming more aware of what we eat, and where it comes from, so a vegetarian diet is becoming the first choice for many people. Research shows that a varied, well-balanced vegetarian diet comes with many health benefits such as reduced risk of coronary artery disease, diabetes and obesity. The beauty of the recipes in this book is their ability to show off the great qualities of grains, pulses, vegetables and dairy foods, demonstrating the health benefits of having one or two vegetarian meals each week.

A proper well-balanced vegetarian diet will provide all the essential nutrients for a long and healthy life:

PROTEIN The human body needs protein as an energy source to help build muscle, brain-cells, hair and nails. Studies show that as little as one serving a day will help to reduce chronic health risks such as a stroke, type 2 diabetes, as well as better weight management. Meat, poultry and fish are not the only sources of protein – grains, eggs, dairy food, nuts, seeds, legumes and soy products are all rich in protein. Whole grains such as quinoa,

barley and brown rice, as well as wholemeal pasta and bread, are great sources of protein. These can easily be added to any of the recipes in this book.

IRON The primary role of iron is to transport oxygen to all parts of the body through the blood. Vegetarians are often thought to be iron-deficient but this is not the case if a well-balanced vegetarian diet is followed. Nuts, soy products, lentils, oats, dried fruits and dark leafy green vegetables such as spinach are all iron-rich options for vegetarians. To help your body absorb the iron, make sure you consume vitamin C at the same time foods such as tomatoes and broccoli or a small glass of freshly-squeezed orange juice.

CALCIUM According to the Australian Nutritional Survey, about 90% of women and 70% of children do not achieve the recommended dietary intake (RDI) for calcium. Calcium is essential for healthy teeth and bones, and helps maintain the health and functioning of muscle tissue and nerves. Dairy products are the main source of calcium. Other calcium-rich ingredients include soy products such as tofu, nuts, seeds, beans and rice milk.

By enjoying a calcium-rich diet, you help reduce the risk of developing osteoporosis.

Our aim is not to turn everyone into a vegetarian, but to help improve overall health by regularly eating meat-free meals.

mini sweet capsicum
fennel
borlotti beans
wombok
zucchini flowers
flat mushroom
shimeji mushrooms
chestnut mushrooms
swiss brown

vegetables

From the everyday to the exotic, there is an abundant variety of vegies to cook with.

red quinoa
red kidney beans
white quinoa
split peas
black-eyed beans

pulses & grains

These humble foods have been popular with cooks for many generations.

panko breadcrumbs
chillies
fresh rice noodles
saffron threads
ginger
kaffir lime leaves
labne
thai basil

special ingredients

These unique ingredients from around the world add wonderful flavour to any dish.

soups

A bowl of hot soup makes for a delicious dinner and an easy lunch the following day. Serve with crusty bread as an added bonus.

spiced carrot soup with smoked almonds

1 tablespoon extra virgin olive oil
2 medium brown onions (300g), chopped coarsely
4cm (1½-inch) piece fresh ginger (20g), grated finely
2 teaspoons ground cumin
1 teaspoon ground coriander
½ cinnamon stick
1kg (2 pounds) carrots, cut into 1cm (½-inch) rounds
2 cups (500ml) vegetable stock
3 cups (750ml) water
¾ cup (200g) Greek-style yoghurt
2 cloves garlic, crushed
½ small red onion (50g), sliced thinly lengthways
¼ cup (40g) chopped smoked almonds
8 sprigs fresh coriander (cilantro)

1 Heat oil in a large saucepan over medium heat; cook brown onion, stirring, until soft.

2 Add ginger, cumin, ground coriander and cinnamon to the pan; cook, stirring, until fragrant. Add carrot, stock and the water; bring to the boil. Reduce heat; simmer, covered, 20 minutes or until soft. Remove cinnamon stick. Stand soup 10 minutes.

3 Meanwhile, combine yoghurt and garlic in a small bowl.

4 Blend soup in batches until smooth (or use a stick blender). Return soup to the pan; stir over medium heat until hot. Season.

5 Ladle soup into serving bowls; top with yoghurt mixture, red onion, nuts and fresh coriander.

prep + cook time 45 minutes **serves** 4
nutritional count per serving 14.5g total fat (3.3g saturated fat); 1190kJ (284 cal); 24g carbohydrate; 8.9g protein; 11.7g fibre

saffron potato soup with capsicum and almonds

- 1 tablespoon extra virgin olive oil
- 2 medium brown onions (300g), chopped finely
- 4 cloves garlic, crushed
- pinch saffron threads
- 5 medium old potatoes (1kg), chopped coarsely
- 3 cups (750ml) vegetable stock
- 3 cups (750ml) water
- 2 tablespoons blanched almonds
- ⅔ cup (150g) capsicum dip

1 Heat oil in a large saucepan over medium heat; cook onion, stirring, until soft. Add garlic and saffron; cook, stirring, until fragrant.
2 Add potatoes to the pan with stock and the water; simmer, covered, 20 minutes or until soft. Stand 10 minutes.
3 Meanwhile, add nuts to a small frying pan; stir over medium heat until toasted lightly. Cool; chop coarsely.
4 Blend soup in batches until smooth (or use a stick blender). Return soup to the pan; stir over medium heat until hot. Season to taste.
5 Ladle soup into serving bowls; top with dip, nuts and freshly ground black pepper.

prep + cook time 50 minutes **serves** 4
nutritional count per serving 11.8g total fat (3.3g saturated fat); 1235kJ (295 cal); 33.3g carbohydrate; 10.1g protein; 6.7g fibre
tips Starchy potatoes such as sebago are suitable for this recipe. This soup is suitable to freeze. Top with dip and almonds after reheating.

greek lima bean soup with fetta and olives

- 2 tablespoons extra virgin olive oil
- 1 large brown onion (200g), chopped coarsely
- 2 medium carrots (240g), chopped coarsely
- 1 stick celery (150g), trimmed, chopped coarsely
- 2 cloves garlic, crushed
- 800g (1½ pounds) canned diced tomatoes
- 1 litre (4 cups) vegetable stock
- 2 cups (500ml) water
- 800g (1½ pounds) canned lima beans, drained, rinsed
- 2 medium green zucchini (240g), halved lengthways, sliced thinly
- 1 teaspoon finely grated lemon rind
- ⅓ cup (50g) seeded kalamata olives, chopped coarsely
- 100g (3 ounces) Greek-style fetta
- 1 tablespoon chopped fresh dill

1 Heat half the oil in a large saucepan over medium heat; cook onion, carrot and celery, stirring, 5 minutes or until softened. Add garlic; cook, stirring, until fragrant.
2 Add tomatoes to pan with stock and the water; bring to the boil. Add beans; simmer, covered, 10 minutes. Add zucchini; simmer, uncovered, about 5 minutes or until tender. Stir in rind; season to taste.
3 Ladle soup into serving bowls; top with olives, crumbled fetta and dill. Drizzle with remaining oil.

prep + cook time 30 minutes **serves** 6
nutritional count per serving 9.7g total fat (3.4g saturated fat); 815kJ (195 cal); 14.1g carbohydrate; 9.1g protein; 7.2g fibre
tips Large canned lima beans are also known as butter beans. Soup can be frozen at the end of step 2.
serving suggestion Warm pitta or crusty bread.

saffron potato soup with capsicum and almonds

greek lima bean soup with fetta and olives

corn soup with parmesan crisps and chilli

8 cobs trimmed corn (2kg)

1 large brown onion (200g), chopped finely

30g (1 ounce) butter

2 cups (500ml) vegetable stock

1 cup (250ml) water

1 cup (250ml) thickened (heavy) cream

1 tablespoon vegetable oil

1 fresh long red chilli, sliced thinly

⅔ cup (10g) puffed corn

fresh baby coriander (cilantro) leaves

parmesan crisps

⅓ cup (25g) finely grated parmesan

1 Cut kernels from corn cobs.

2 Heat butter in a large saucepan over medium heat; cook onion, stirring, until soft but not coloured. Add stock and the water; bring to the boil. Add corn kernels; simmer, covered, 20 minutes or until corn is tender. Stand 10 minutes.

3 Meanwhile, make parmesan crisps.

4 Blend half the soup mixture until smooth; return to the pan. Stir in cream over medium heat until hot. Season to taste.

5 Heat oil in a small frying pan; cook chilli, stirring, until soft.

6 Ladle soup into serving bowls; top with puffed corn, chilli and the oil, then coriander. Serve with parmesan crisps.

parmesan crisps Preheat oven to 180°C/350°F. Line a large oven tray with baking paper. Sprinkle parmesan in a thin layer on tray; flatten slightly. Bake 8 minutes or until browned lightly. Cool on tray. Break into pieces when cold.

prep + cook time 40 minutes **serves** 4

nutritional count per serving 40.1g total fat (20.7g saturated fat); 2503kJ (598 cal); 37.6g carbohydrate; 15.2g protein; 15.1g fibre

tip You can use 1.6kg (11 cups) frozen corn kernels to save time.

mushroom soup with herbed goat's cheese croûtes

- 40g (1½ ounces) butter
- 1 tablespoon extra virgin olive oil
- 1 large brown onion (200g), chopped
- 200g (6½ ounces) swiss brown mushrooms, sliced thinly
- 500g (1 pound) cup mushrooms, sliced thinly
- 2 cloves garlic, crushed
- 1 teaspoon chopped fresh thyme leaves
- 1 litre (4 cups) vegetable stock
- 2 cups (500ml) water
- 100g (3 ounces) baby spinach leaves

herbed goat's cheese croûtes

- 8 x 1.5cm (¾-inch) thick slices sourdough bread (320g)
- 120g (4 ounces) soft goat's cheese
- 1 clove garlic, crushed
- 1 tablespoon chopped fresh chives
- 1 tablespoon chopped fresh flat-leaf parsley
- 1 teaspoon chopped fresh thyme leaves

1 Heat butter and oil in a large saucepan over medium heat; cook onion, stirring, 5 minutes or until soft but not browned.
2 Increase heat to high. Add mushrooms to the pan; cook, stirring, 5 minutes or until well browned. Add garlic and thyme; cook, stirring, until fragrant. Stir in stock and the water; simmer, covered, 15 minutes or until tender.
3 Meanwhile, make herbed goat's cheese croûtes.
4 Add spinach to soup, stir until wilted. Season to taste.
5 Ladle soup into serving bowls; sprinkle with a few extra thyme sprigs. Serve with croûtes.

herbed goat's cheese croûtes Preheat grill (broiler). Place bread under grill until toasted lightly on both sides. Combine cheese, garlic and herbs in a small bowl; spread herbed cheese mixture on toast.

prep + cook time 35 minutes **serves** 4
nutritional count per serving 23.1g total fat (10.9g saturated fat); 2082kJ (497 cal); 46.5g carbohydrate; 22.5g protein; 8.2g fibre
tip This soup is not suitable to freeze.

primavera soup with pangrattato

30g (1 ounce) butter

4 shallots (100g), chopped

1 litre (4 cups) vegetable stock

2 cups (500ml) water

⅓ cup (75g) risoni pasta

250g (8 ounces) baby green zucchini, halved lengthways

150g (4½ ounces) asparagus, cut into 3cm (1¼-inch) lengths

2 cups (240g) frozen baby peas

pangrattato

200g (6½ ounces) crusty italian bread

2 tablespoons extra virgin olive oil

1 fresh long red chilli, sliced thinly

2 cloves garlic, chopped

⅓ cup loosely packed small fresh flat-leaf parsley leaves

1 teaspoon finely grated lemon rind

1 Heat butter in a large saucepan over medium heat; cook shallots, stirring, 3 minutes or until soft.

2 Add stock and the water to pan; bring to the boil. Add pasta and zucchini; simmer, uncovered, 5 minutes, stirring occasionally.

3 Meanwhile, make pangrattato.

4 Add asparagus and peas to soup; simmer, uncovered, 5 minutes or until just tender. Season to taste.

5 Ladle soup into serving bowls; top with pangrattato.

pangrattato Remove crust from bread; tear into 1cm (½-inch) pieces. Heat oil in a large frying pan over medium-high heat; cook chilli and bread pieces, stirring, until browned lightly and crisp. Add garlic; cook until fragrant. Remove from heat; stir in parsley and rind. Season to taste.

prep + cook time 25 minutes **serves** 4

nutritional count per serving 17.7g total fat (5.9g saturated fat); 1760kJ (420 cal); 46.7g carbohydrate; 14.3g protein; 9.2g fibre

tips This soup is best made just before serving as it will discolour on standing.

If you can't find baby zucchini, use medium-sized zucchini sliced thinly.

chinese noodle, tofu and vegetable soup

1 litre (4 cups) vegetable stock

1 litre (4 cups) water

4cm (1½-inch) piece fresh ginger (20g), grated finely

1 clove garlic, crushed

¼ cup (60ml) light soy sauce

1 teaspoon white (granulated) sugar

100g (3 ounces) fresh shiitake mushrooms

300g (9½ ounces) gai lan

450g (14½ ounces) fresh hokkien noodles

1 medium carrot (120g), cut into long thin strips

1 stick celery (150g), trimmed, cut into long thin strips

300g (9½ ounces) silken tofu

½ teaspoon sesame oil

1 fresh long red chilli, sliced thinly

2 green onions (scallions), sliced thinly

pinch ground white pepper

1 Bring stock, the water, ginger, garlic, sauce and sugar to the boil in a large saucepan.

2 Meanwhile, remove stems from mushrooms; thinly slice caps. Separate gai lan stems and leaves.

3 Rinse noodles under warm water to separate; drain well.

4 Add carrot, celery, mushrooms, gai lan stems and noodles to the pan; simmer, uncovered, 2 minutes. Add gai lan leaves; simmer, uncovered, 1 minute or until just tender.

5 Cut tofu into 1.5cm (¾-inch) cubes; add to soup with oil. Season to taste with a little extra soy sauce or salt. Remove from heat.

6 Ladle soup into serving bowls; top with chilli, green onion and white pepper.

prep + cook time 20 minutes **serves** 4

nutritional count per serving 5.7g total fat (0.8g saturated fat); 1414kJ (338 cal); 50.4g carbohydrate; 18.4g protein; 6g fibre

tip This soup is best made close to serving.

curried kumara and lentil soup

- ½ cup (100g) red lentils
- 1 tablespoon vegetable oil
- 1 large brown onion (200g), chopped coarsely
- 1 teaspoon cumin seeds
- 1 teaspoon brown mustard seeds
- ¼ cup (75g) madras curry paste
- 6 curry leaves
- 2 cups (500ml) coconut cream
- 1 litre (4 cups) vegetable stock
- 1 cup (250ml) water
- 1kg (2 pounds) kumara (orange sweet potato)
- ¼ cup loosely packed fresh coriander (cilantro) sprigs
- ¼ cup loosely packed fresh mint leaves, torn
- 1 medium lemon (140g), cut into wedges

1 Place lentils in a medium bowl; cover with cold water. Stir well. Remove any lentils that float to the surface. Drain well.
2 Heat oil in a large saucepan over medium heat; cook onion, stirring, until soft. Add seeds, paste and leaves; cook, stirring, until fragrant.
3 Reserve 2 tablespoons coconut cream. Stir remaining coconut cream into the pan with stock and the water; bring to the boil.
4 Meanwhile, chop kumara into 1.5cm (¾-inch) pieces. Add to the pan; simmer, covered, 10 minutes. Add lentils to the pan; simmer, covered, further 10 minutes or until tender. Season to taste. Remove curry leaves. Break up most of the kumara with a wooden spoon.
5 Ladle soup into serving bowls; top with reserved coconut cream, coriander sprigs and mint. Serve with lemon wedges.

prep + cook time 35 minutes **serves** 4
nutritional count per serving 35.8g total fat (23.1g saturated fat); 2542kJ (607 cal); 51.9g carbohydrate; 16.1g protein; 11.2g fibre
serving suggestion Pappadums or chapatti.

spiced chickpea and broad bean soup with eggs and cumin salt

1 tablespoon extra virgin olive oil
1 medium brown onion (150g), chopped coarsely
2 medium carrots (240g), chopped coarsely
2 sticks celery (300g), trimmed, chopped coarsely
2 cloves garlic, chopped
2 teaspoons ground cumin
2 teaspoons ground coriander
2 teaspoons paprika
½ teaspoon ground cinnamon
400g (12½ ounces) canned diced tomatoes
1.5 litres (6 cups) vegetable stock
½ cup (100g) French-style green lentils, rinsed
400g (12½ ounces) canned chickpeas (garbanzo beans), drained, rinsed
2 cups (320g) frozen broad (fava) beans
¼ cup coarsely chopped fresh flat-leaf parsley
¼ cup coarsely chopped fresh coriander (cilantro)
4 eggs
¼ teaspoon ground cumin, extra
½ teaspoon sea salt flakes
1 medium lemon (140g), cut into wedges

1 Heat oil in a large saucepan over medium heat; cook onion, carrot, celery and garlic, stirring, 5 minutes or until softened. Add spices; cook, stirring, until fragrant.
2 Add tomatoes and stock; bring to the boil. Add lentils and chickpeas; simmer, uncovered, 10 minutes.
3 Meanwhile, pour boiling water over broad beans in a heatproof bowl; stand 2 minutes, drain. Peel broad beans.
4 Add broad beans to the pan; simmer, uncovered, further 5 minutes or until lentils are tender. Stir in half the herbs; season to taste.
5 Meanwhile, place eggs in a small saucepan; cover with cold water. Bring to the boil; simmer, uncovered, 3 minutes. Drain; run under cold water until cool enough to handle. Peel eggs; chop coarsely.
6 Ladle soup into serving bowls; top with egg, remaining herbs and combined extra cumin and salt. Serve with lemon wedges.

prep + cook time 35 minutes **serves** 6
nutritional count per serving 9.1g total fat (2g saturated fat); 1103kJ (263 cal); 23.1g carbohydrate; 17.6g protein; 11.7g fibre
tip This soup can be prepared to the end of step 3 up to 6 hours ahead.
serving suggestion Warm afghani or turkish bread.

fennel and tomato soup with rouille

1 medium leek (350g)

1 large fennel (550g)

¼ cup (60ml) extra virgin olive oil

1 medium brown onion (150g), chopped coarsely

1 stick celery (150g), trimmed, chopped coarsely

3 cloves garlic, crushed

pinch saffron threads

800g (1½ pounds) canned diced tomatoes

1 litre (4 cups) vegetable stock

2 medium brushed potatoes (400g), cut into 1.5cm (¾-inch) pieces

8 x 1.5cm (¾-inch) thick slices sourdough bread (380g)

rouille

⅔ cup (200g) whole-egg mayonnaise

3 teaspoons lemon juice

3 teaspoons tomato paste

2 cloves garlic, crushed

pinch saffron threads

¼ teaspoon cayenne pepper

1 Quarter leek lengthways; slice thinly. Reserve fennel tops; chop fennel finely.

2 Heat half the oil in a large saucepan over medium-high heat; cook leek, onion, celery and fennel, stirring, 5 minutes or until softened. Add garlic and saffron; cook, stirring, until fragrant. Add tomatoes, stock and potatoes; bring to the boil. Reduce heat; simmer, covered, 10 minutes or until tender. Season to taste. Cover to keep hot.

3 Meanwhile, make rouille.

4 Heat a grill pan (or grill or barbecue). Brush bread on both sides with remaining oil; cook until browned lightly on both sides.

5 Ladle soup into serving bowls; top with reserved fennel tops. Serve with toasted bread and rouille.

rouille Combine ingredients in a small bowl; season to taste.

prep + cook time 30 minutes **serves** 4

nutritional count per serving 58.3g total fat (9.4g saturated fat); 3825kJ (914 cal); 74.4g carbohydrate; 17.8g protein; 13g fibre

tip This soup can be frozen at the end of step 2. Rouille can be made a day ahead.

ratatouille soup with pistou

2 tablespoons extra virgin olive oil

2 medium red onions (340g), chopped

1 medium eggplant (300g), chopped

2 medium red capsicums (bell peppers) (400g), chopped

4 cloves garlic, chopped

2 medium green zucchini (240g), chopped

800g (1½ pounds) canned diced tomatoes

1 litre (4 cups) vegetable stock

2 x 110g (3½-ounce) mini baguettes

300g (9½ ounces) ricotta

½ cup (40g) finely grated parmesan

pistou

2 cloves garlic, peeled

¼ cup (60ml) extra virgin olive oil

1 cup loosely packed fresh basil leaves

1 Heat oil in a large saucepan over medium heat; cook onion, stirring, 5 minutes or until soft. Add eggplant, capsicum and garlic; cook, covered, over low heat, 20 minutes or until soft.

2 Add zucchini, tomatoes and stock; simmer, covered, 10 minutes or until zucchini is tender. Season to taste.

3 Meanwhile, make pistou.

4 Preheat grill (broiler).

5 Split bread lengthways, then in half crossways. Spread with 2 tablespoons of the pistou then ricotta; sprinkle with parmesan. Place on an oven tray under the grill until browned lightly.

6 Ladle soup into serving bowls; top with remaining pistou. Serve with bread.

pistou Blend or process garlic, oil and basil in small processor or food mill until almost smooth. Season to taste. Transfer to a small bowl; cover tightly with plastic wrap.

prep + cook time 45 minutes **serves** 6

nutritional count per serving 23.3g total fat (6.5g saturated fat); 1759kJ (420 cal); 33.3g carbohydrate; 16.1g protein; 7.4g fibre

tip This soup is not suitable to freeze.

vegetable laksa with fried tofu

250g (8 ounces) dried vermicelli noodles

2 cups (500ml) coconut milk

1 litre (4 cups) vegetable stock

1 cup (250ml) water

125g (4 ounces) baby corn, halved lengthways

75g (2½ ounces) snow peas, halved lengthways

200g (6½ ounces) fried tofu puffs, halved

1 cup (80g) bean sprouts

¼ cup lightly packed fresh coriander (cilantro) sprigs

1 tablespoon sambal oelek

1 medium lime (90g), cut into wedges

vegetarian laksa paste

1 tablespoon peanut or vegetable oil

6cm (2½-inch) piece fresh ginger (30g), chopped

1 fresh kaffir lime leaf, rib removed

4 fresh coriander (cilantro) roots, cleaned

10cm (4-inch) stick fresh lemon grass (20g), chopped coarsely

1 small red onion (100g), chopped coarsely

2 teaspoons salt

2 fresh small red chillies

4 cloves garlic, peeled

2 teaspoons ground coriander

1 teaspoon ground turmeric

1 teaspoon paprika

¼ cup (35g) macadamias

2 teaspoons brown sugar

1 Make vegetarian laksa paste.

2 Place noodles in a heatproof bowl; cover with boiling water. Stand 5 minutes; drain.

3 Cook laksa paste in a large saucepan over low heat, stirring, 5 minutes or until fragrant. Stir in coconut milk, stock and the water; simmer, uncovered, 5 minutes. Add corn and snow peas; simmer, uncovered, until just tender. Add tofu; simmer, uncovered, until hot. Season to taste.

4 Divide noodles between serving bowls. Ladle soup mixture over noodles; top with bean sprouts and coriander sprigs. Serve with sambal oelek and lime wedges.

vegetarian laksa paste Blend or process ingredients until mixture forms a paste.

prep + cook time 35 minutes **serves** 4

nutritional count per serving 36.7g total fat (20.2g saturated fat); 2013kJ (482 cal); 25.9g carbohydrate; 13.9g protein; 8.2g fibre

tip Laksa paste can be made 2 days ahead; keep tightly covered in the refrigerator. Soup is not suitable to freeze.

tom yum soup

2 tablespoons vegetable oil

5cm (2-inch) piece fresh ginger (25g), grated finely

1 clove garlic, crushed

2 x 20cm (8-inch) sticks lemon grass (40g), chopped finely

2 fresh long red chillies, chopped finely

2 green onions (scallions), sliced thinly

100g (3 ounces) fresh shiitake mushrooms, sliced thickly

125g (4 ounces) cherry tomatoes, halved

2 teaspoons finely grated palm sugar

¼ cup (60ml) soy sauce

¼ cup (60ml) lime juice

2 cups (160g) bean sprouts

¼ cup loosely packed fresh coriander (cilantro) leaves

stock

1 fresh long red chilli, sliced thinly

2 green onions (scallions), sliced thinly

1 cup lightly packed fresh coriander (cilantro) leaves, sliced thinly

5cm (2-inch) piece fresh ginger (25g), grated finely

6 fresh kaffir lime leaves, torn

2 tablespoons tomato paste

1 tablespoon finely grated lime rind

2 litres (8 cups) water

2 cups (500ml) vegetable stock

1 Make stock.

2 Heat oil in a large saucepan over medium heat; cook ginger, garlic, lemon grass and half the chilli, stirring, 3 minutes or until fragrant. Add mushrooms; cook, stirring, 2 minutes.

3 Stir in stock, tomatoes, onion, sugar and sauce; bring to the boil. Reduce heat; simmer 5 minutes.

4 Just before serving, stir in juice. Ladle soup into serving bowls; top with combined bean sprouts, coriander and remaining chilli.

stock Place ingredients in a large saucepan; bring to the boil. Reduce heat; simmer, uncovered, 20 minutes, using a large ladle to skim any scum from surface of stock. Remove from heat. Strain stock through a fine sieve into a jug or heatproof bowl; discard solids. You will need 3 litres (12 cups) stock.

prep + cook time 40 minutes **serves** 4

nutritional count per serving 10.3g total fat (1.3g saturated fat); 603kJ (144 cal); 7g carbohydrate; 4.8g protein; 2.9g fibre

tip You will need about 3 limes for this recipe.

barley and vegetable soup with crunchy seeds

2 tablespoons extra virgin olive oil
1 large red onion (300g), chopped
1 medium parsnip (250g), chopped
2 sticks celery (300g), trimmed, chopped
4 cloves garlic, chopped
1 cup (250ml) bottled tomato pasta sauce (passata)
1 litre (4 cups) vegetable stock
1 litre (4 cups) water
2 medium red capsicum (bell peppers) (400g), chopped
400g (12½ ounces) canned cannellini beans, drained, rinsed
½ cup (100g) pearl barley or spelt, rinsed
2 tablespoons pepitas (pumpkin seed kernels)
2 tablespoons sunflower seeds
2 tablespoons drained baby capers, rinsed
2 tablespoons dried currants
¼ cup loosely packed torn fresh basil leaves
½ cup (40g) finely grated parmesan

1 Heat half the oil in a large saucepan over medium heat; cook onion, parsnip, celery and garlic, stirring, 5 minutes or until softened.
2 Add sauce, stock and the water; bring to the boil. Stir in capsicum, beans and barley; simmer, covered, 25 minutes or until barley is tender. Season to taste.
3 Meanwhile, heat remaining oil in a small frying pan over medium-high heat; cook seeds and capers, stirring, until browned lightly and fragrant. Add currants; stir until combined.
4 Just before serving, stir basil into soup. Ladle soup into serving bowls; sprinkle with seed mixture and parmesan.

prep + cook time 45 minutes **serves** 6
nutritional count per serving 11.1g total fat (2.7g saturated fat); 1244kJ (298 cal); 34.2g carbohydrate; 11.8g protein; 9.2g fibre
tip This soup, without seed topping, can be frozen for up to 3 months. Add a little extra water on reheating, if needed.

spinach, rocket and pea soup with brie croûtes

- 40g (1½ ounces) butter
- 1 medium leek (350g), sliced
- 1 clove garlic, crushed
- 1 large brushed potato (300g), chopped
- 1 litre (4 cups) vegetable stock
- 1 cup (250ml) water
- 1 cup (120g) frozen peas
- 270g (8½ ounces) spinach, trimmed
- 30g (1 ounce) firmly packed baby rocket (arugula)
- ½ cup (125ml) pouring cream

brie croûtes

- 12 slices sourdough baguette (120g)
- 1 tablespoon dijon mustard
- 150g (4½ ounces) brie cheese

1 Heat butter in a large saucepan over medium heat; cook leek, stirring, 5 minutes or until soft but not coloured. Add garlic; cook, stirring, until fragrant.

2 Add potato, stock and the water to the pan; bring to the boil. Reduce heat; simmer, uncovered, 10 minutes or until potato is tender. Add peas, spinach and rocket; simmer, uncovered, 5 minutes. Remove from heat; stand soup 5 minutes.

3 Blend soup in batches until smooth. Return soup to a cleaned pan; stir in cream until hot over medium heat. Season to taste.

4 Meanwhile, make brie croûtes.

5 Ladle soup into serving bowls; serve with croûtes and freshly ground black pepper.

brie croûtes Preheat grill (broiler) to high. Place bread under grill until browned lightly on one side. Turn bread, spread with mustard and top with slices of cheese. Grill until melted slightly.

prep + cook time 35 minutes **serves** 4

nutritional count per serving 33.2g total fat (20.4g saturated fat); 2088kJ (500 cal); 29.5g carbohydrate; 18g protein; 7.3g fibre

tips A blender will produce a smoother, finer textured soup than a food processor.

This soup is suitable to freeze.

salads

For fresh, fabulous salads that are packed with vegies, look no further. Try a colourful jewelled couscous or greenest green salad.

jewelled couscous salad

- 180g (5½ ounces) persian fetta in oil
- 1½ cups (300g) couscous
- 1½ cups (375ml) boiling water
- ½ cup (70g) shelled pistachios
- ½ cup loosely packed fresh coriander (cilantro) leaves, chopped coarsely
- ½ cup loosely packed fresh flat-leaf parsley leaves, chopped coarsely
- 3 green onions (scallions), sliced thinly
- ⅓ cup (50g) raisins
- ¼ cup (60ml) lemon juice
- 1 teaspoon sumac
- ⅓ cup (70g) pomegranate seeds

1 Drain oil from fetta into a jug or bowl; you will need ¼ cup of the oil for this recipe.
2 Combine couscous with the boiling water and 1 tablespoon of the fetta oil in a large heatproof bowl, cover; stand 5 minutes or until liquid is absorbed, fluffing occasionally with a fork.
3 Meanwhile, place nuts in a small frying pan; stir over medium heat until toasted lightly. Transfer nuts to a chopping board, cool slightly; chop coarsely. Stir nuts, herbs, onion and raisins into couscous; season to taste.
4 Whisk remaining fetta oil in a jug or small bowl with juice and sumac; season to taste.
5 Add dressing and pomegranate seeds to salad; toss gently to combine.
6 Transfer salad to a platter; top with crumbled fetta. Sprinkle with a little extra sumac.

prep + cook time 15 minutes **serves** 4
nutritional count per serving 33.4g total fat (9.8g saturated fat); 2805kJ (670 cal); 70g carbohydrate; 18.8g protein; 8.3g fibre
tips Fresh pomegranate seeds can sometimes be found in packs in the fridge section of supermarkets or good green grocers. If unavailable, break a medium pomegranate in half, then turn one half upside down over a bowl. Hit the shell with a wooden spoon – the seeds usually fall out easily. If they don't, dig them out with a spoon. Repeat with the other half. This recipe can be made several hours ahead; add dressing close to serving.

greenest green salad

5 slices multi-grain bread (180g)

150g (4½ ounces) green beans, trimmed

170g (5½ ounces) asparagus, halved lengthways if large

⅔ cup (80g) frozen peas

1 medium ripe avocado (250g)

2 tablespoons lemon juice

½ cup (130g) basil pesto

1 tablespoon water

3 cups (90g) loosely packed trimmed watercress sprigs

1 Preheat a grill plate (or grill or barbecue) over medium-high heat. Remove crusts from bread and tear into bite-sized pieces. Toast bread on the grill plate 1 minute or until golden.

2 Add beans to a medium saucepan of boiling salted water; boil, uncovered, 1 minute. Add asparagus to the same pan; boil 1½ minutes. Add peas; boil for a further 30 seconds or until bright green. Drain; place in a large bowl of iced water to cool. Drain well.

3 Cut avocado in half, remove seed. Squeeze flesh out of each half; drizzle with 1 tablespoon of the juice.

4 Place pesto in a large bowl; stir in water and remaining juice. Add bread, beans, asparagus and peas, then watercress; toss gently to coat. Season to taste.

5 Transfer salad to a serving platter; top with avocado.

prep + cook time 15 minutes **serves** 4

nutritional count per serving 22.5g total fat (4.1g saturated fat); 1360kJ (325 cal); 19g carbohydrate; 8.7g protein; 7g fibre

tips Any flavoured pesto can be used in place of basil pesto. You will need a bunch of watercress that weighs about 350g (11 ounces).

grape and apple salad with goat's cheese

500g (1 pound) red seedless grapes

2 large green-skinned apples (400g)

¼ cup (60ml) lemon juice

½ cup (50g) walnuts

120g (4 ounces) goat's cheese, crumbled

3 cups (90g) loosely packed trimmed watercress sprigs

1 cup loosely packed fresh flat-leaf parsley leaves

¼ cup (60ml) olive oil

½ medium lemon (70g), cut into wedges

1 Halve grapes. Thinly slice apples into rounds on a mandoline or V-slicer. Place grapes and apple in a large bowl wtih juice; toss gently to combine. Cover.

2 Stir nuts in a small frying pan over medium heat until toasted lightly. Cool; chop coarsely.

3 Place apple and grape mixture on platter; top with cheese, nuts, watercress, parsley and oil. Serve with lemon wedges.

prep + cook time 20 minutes **serves** 4

nutritional count per serving 28.9g total fat (7g saturated fat); 1797kJ (430 cal); 30.1g carbohydrate; 9.9g protein; 8.1g fibre

tip You will need a bunch of watercress that weighs about 350g (11 ounces).

serving suggestion Serve with grilled bruschetta.

ruby grapefruit, orange and basil salad

⅔ cup (160ml) balsamic vinegar

⅓ cup (75g) firmly packed brown sugar

6 small ruby grapefruit (1.5kg)

4 medium oranges (960g)

½ cup (60g) pecans

100g (3 ounces) fetta

1 cup loosely packed fresh basil leaves

1 Preheat oven to 200°C/400°F.

2 Cook vinegar and half the sugar in a small saucepan over medium heat, stirring, until sugar dissolves; bring to the boil. Reduce heat; simmer, uncovered, 15 minutes or until large bubbles form and mixture is reduced by half. Cool.

3 Meanwhile, peel grapefruit and oranges thickly, removing all white pith. Thinly slice grapefruit and oranges.

4 Stir nuts in a small frying pan over medium heat until toasted lightly. Cool; chop coarsely.

5 Arrange orange slices on a large serving platter; top with crumbled fetta, nuts and basil. Sprinkle with remaining sugar then drizzle with balsamic dressing just before serving.

prep + cook time 35 minutes **serves** 6

nutritional count per serving 11.5g total fat (3g saturated fat); 1136kJ (272 cal); 33g carbohydrate; 6.8g protein; 4.9g fibre

grape and apple salad with goat's cheese

ruby grapefruit, orange and basil salad

crunchy mung bean and coriander salad

2 tablespoons sunflower seeds

2 tablespoons pepitas (pumpkin seed kernels)

85g (3 ounces) fresh coriander (cilantro), roots and stems attached

3 green onions (scallions), sliced thinly

¼ teaspoon ground coriander

¼ teaspoon ground cumin

¼ cup (60ml) extra virgin olive oil

¼ cup (60ml) lime juice

2 lebanese cucumbers (260g)

2 medium roma (egg) tomatoes (150g)

400g (12½ ounces) crunchy combo sprouted legumes

1 Stir seeds in a small frying pan, over medium heat, until toasted lightly. Cool.

2 Wash fresh coriander well; drain and pat dry. Reserve 1 cup lightly packed coriander leaves. Scrape and clean coriander roots. Blend or process coriander roots, stems and remaining coriander leaves with one-third of the onion, spices, oil and juice; process until finely chopped. Season to taste.

3 Halve cucumbers and tomatoes; remove seeds, then cut into 1cm (½-inch) pieces.

4 Place seeds, coriander dressing, cucumber and tomato in a large bowl with sprouts and remaining onion, spices, oil and juice; toss gently to combine. Season to taste. Serve immediately.

prep + cook time 10 minutes **serves** 6

nutritional count per serving 12.7g total fat (2.1g saturated fat); 634kJ (151 cal); 3.6g carbohydrate; 4.9g protein; 4.4g fibre

tip The dressing discolours quickly, so make the dressing close to serving.

serving suggestion Crusty bread.

lentil, gorgonzola and witlof salad

½ cup (100g) French-style green lentils

¾ cup (75g) walnuts

½ cup (125ml) sherry or red wine vinegar

½ cup (125ml) extra virgin olive oil

1 small radicchio (150g), leaves separated

2 large witlof (belgian endive) (250g), leaves separated

180g (5½ ounces) grape tomatoes, halved if large

1 cup loosely packed fresh flat-leaf parsley leaves

120g (4 ounces) gorgonzola

1 Cook lentils in a medium saucepan of boiling water, uncovered, 25 minutes or until lentils are tender; drain. Rinse under cold water; drain well.

2 Meanwhile, add nuts to a small frying pan; stir over medium heat until nuts are toasted lightly. Transfer to a chopping board, cool slightly; chop coarsely.

3 Whisk vinegar and oil in a large serving bowl; season to taste. Add radicchio, witlof, tomatoes, parsley and lentils; toss gently to combine. Sprinkle with nuts and crumbled gorgonzola.

prep + cook time 30 minutes **serves** 4

nutritional count per serving 49.6g total fat (9.9g saturated fat); 2379kJ (568 cal); 9.9g carbohydrate; 13.2g protein; 11.1g fibre

tips Canned brown lentils can be used in place of French-style green lentils to save time.

Radicchio and witlof have a bitter flavour. You can use baby cos (romaine) lettuce if you prefer. You could use cherry tomatoes if grape tomatoes are unavailable.

baby beetroot, green lentil, watercress and hazelnut salad

- 1kg (2 pounds) baby beetroot (beets)
- 2 cloves garlic, sliced
- ¼ cup loosely packed fresh rosemary leaves
- 2 tablespoons extra virgin olive oil
- ¼ cup (60ml) balsamic vinegar
- ½ cup (100g) French-style green lentils
- 1 large pomegranate (430g)
- 100g (3 ounces) trimmed watercress
- ⅓ cup (45g) roasted hazelnuts, chopped coarsely

1 Preheat oven to 200°C/400°F.

2 Trim beetroot tops to 4cm (1½ inches); halve beetroot, or quarter if large. Place beetroot, garlic and rosemary in a large baking dish; drizzle with oil and vinegar. Roast, uncovered, 30 minutes or until tender.

3 Meanwhile, cook lentils in a medium saucepan of boiling water 25 minutes or until lentils are tender. Drain; rinse under cold water. Drain well.

4 Cut pomegranate in half; turn one half upside down over a small bowl. Hit the shell with a wooden spoon – the seeds should fall out easily. If not, dig them out with a teaspoon. Repeat with remaining half.

5 Place lentils, beetroot and cooking juices, watercress, half the pomegranate seeds and half the nuts in a large bowl, season to taste, toss gently to combine. Transfer to a serving bowl; sprinkle with remaining pomegranate seeds and nuts.

prep + cook time 40 minutes **serves** 4

nutritional count per serving 16.5g total fat (1.9g saturated fat); 1592kJ (380 cal); 38.7g carbohydrate; 9.9g protein; 19.4g fibre

tips If roasted hazelnuts are unavailable, you can roast your own. Place nuts on an oven tray; roast at 200°C/400°F about 5 minutes or until the skins begin to split. Rub hazelnuts in a tea towel to remove most of the skins. Cool.

Fresh pomegranate seeds can sometimes be found in packs in the fridge section of supermarkets or good green grocers.

brussels sprout salad with poached egg

- 2 tablespoons white vinegar
- 4 eggs
- 400g (12½ ounces) brussels sprouts, shredded
- ¼ cup (40g) pine nuts
- ½ cup lightly packed torn fresh basil leaves
- ⅓ cup (25g) shaved parmesan
- ¼ cup (60ml) balsamic vinegar
- 2 tablespoons extra virgin olive oil

1 Add white vinegar to a deep frying pan of simmering water. Break eggs, one at a time, into a cup; slide each egg into the water. Gently poach eggs 3 minutes or until whites are set. Remove from pan with slotted spoon; drain on absorbent paper.
2 Meanwhile, add sprouts to a medium saucepan of boiling salted water; boil 5 seconds. Drain. Place sprouts in a large bowl of iced water; stand until cold. Drain well.
3 Stir pine nuts in a small frying pan over medium heat until toasted lightly.
4 Place sprouts, pine nuts and basil in a medium bowl, season to taste; toss gently to combine.
5 Divide salad between serving bowls, top with poached eggs and parmesan. Drizzle with balsamic vinegar and oil. Season to taste.

prep + cook time 20 minutes **serves** 4
nutritional count per serving 22.7g total fat (4.7g saturated fat); 1263kJ (302 cal); 7.3g carbohydrate; 13.9g protein; 5.2g fibre
tip We used fresh free-range eggs as they have thick egg whites that keep their shape while cooking.

red salad

- ⅔ cup (160ml) tarragon vinegar
- ¼ cup (55g) caster (superfine) sugar
- 1 medium red onion (170g), halved, sliced thinly
- ½ medium red cabbage (750g), shredded finely
- ¼ cup (20g) flaked almonds
- 450g (14½ ounces) canned baby beetroot (beets)
- ¼ cup fresh chives, cut into lengths
- 2 small radicchio (300g), cut into thin wedges
- 150g (4½ ounces) goat's cheese
- 1 tablespoon extra virgin olive oil

1 Whisk vinegar and sugar in a large bowl until sugar is dissolved. Add onion and cabbage; toss gently to coat. Stand 30 minutes to pickle slightly. Drain in a colander; discard excess dressing. Season to taste.
2 Meanwhile, stir nuts in a small frying pan over medium heat until toasted lightly. Cool.
3 Drain beetroot; cut any larger pieces into irregular shapes. Add beetroot and half the chives to cabbage mixture; toss gently to combine.
4 Arrange radicchio on a serving platter; sprinkle with cabbage mixture. Crumble goat's cheese over salad; top with nuts and remaining chives. Drizzle with oil.

prep + cook time 30 minutes (+ standing) **serves** 4
nutritional count per serving 18.1g total fat (6.5g saturated fat); 1350kJ (323 cal); 19.1g carbohydrate; 15.3g protein; 12.2g fibre

brussels sprout salad with poached egg

red salad

fattoush

- 180g (5½ ounces) persian fetta in oil
- 2 tablespoons pomegranate molasses
- 2 tablespoons lemon juice
- 1 baby cos (romaine) lettuce (180g), quartered lengthways
- 1 lebanese cucumber (130g), sliced thinly
- 6 red radishes (300g), sliced thinly
- 3 green onions (scallions), sliced thinly
- 1 medium green capsicum (bell pepper) (200g), cut into 2cm (¾-inch) pieces
- 250g (8 ounces) cherry tomatoes, halved
- ½ cup lightly packed fresh mint leaves
- 1½ cups (45g) pitta crisps
- ½ teaspoon sumac

1 Drain oil from fetta into a jug or small bowl; you will need ¼ cup oil for this recipe.
2 Whisk pomegranate molasses, oil from fetta and juice in a large bowl. Season to taste. Add lettuce, cucumber, radish, onion, capsicum, tomatoes and mint; toss gently to combine.
3 Crumble fetta over salad; top with pitta crisps and sprinkle with sumac.

prep time 10 minutes **serves** 4
nutritional count per serving 20.7g total fat (8.1g saturated fat); 1274kJ (304 cal); 17.7g carbohydrate; 9.1g protein; 4.8g fibre
tips The dressing can be made a day ahead. Assemble the salad just before serving.
Pitta crisps are available from some delis, greengrocers and specialist food stores.

crunchy asian rice salad

2 x 250g (8 ounces) packaged quick-cook brown basmati rice

1 lebanese cucumber (130g)

½ small wombok (napa cabbage) (350g), shredded

100g (3 ounces) snow peas, sliced thinly

1 small carrot (70g), cut into long thin strips

2 cups (160g) bean sprouts

2 green onions (scallions), sliced thinly

½ cup (70g) salted peanuts, chopped coarsely

¼ cup loosely packed fresh perilla leaves

¼ cup loosely packed fresh thai basil leaves

sesame dressing

2 tablespoons kecap manis

¼ cup (70g) tahini

1 teaspoon sesame oil

2 tablespoons mirin

2 tablespoons water

1 Heat rice in a microwave oven according to packet instructions.
2 Meanwhile, halve cucumber lengthways; remove seeds. Cut cucumber into long thin strips.
3 Place rice and cucumber in a large bowl with wombok, snow peas, carrot and sprouts, then most of the onion, peanuts, torn perilla and thai basil; toss gently to combine.
4 Make sesame dressing.
5 Add dressing to salad; toss gently to combine. Top salad with remaining onion, peanuts, perilla and thai basil.
sesame dressing Whisk ingredients together in a small bowl.

prep + cook time 15 minutes **serves** 4
nutritional count per serving 23.1g total fat (3.3g saturated fat); 2201kJ (526 cal); 17.2g carbohydrate; 18.1g protein; 9.5g fibre
tip Perilla leaves, also known as shiso leaves, belong to the mint family and are available in green and purple-red varieties from Asian grocers. Use the leaves whole or shredded, as an ingredient or a condiment. You can use mint leaves instead.

tomato salad with labne and za'atar

- 400g (12½ ounces) mixed tomatoes
- 170g (5½ ounces) grape tomatoes
- 250g (8 ounces) teardrop tomatoes
- 310g (10 ounces) bottled marinated eggplant in oil, drained
- 300g (9½ ounces) labne in chilli, rosemary and garlic oil
- 1 long green chilli, chopped finely
- 1 clove garlic, crushed
- 1½ tablespoons lemon juice
- 3 teaspoons za'atar
- ¼ cup lightly packed fresh mint leaves
- ¼ cup lightly packed fresh flat-leaf parsley leaves

1 Cut tomatoes into irregular shapes, leaving some whole; place in a large bowl.
2 Cut eggplant into bite-sized pieces; add to bowl.
3 Drain labne, reserving ¼ cup of the oil. Whisk reserved oil, chilli, garlic, juice and 2 teaspoons of the za'atar in a small bowl until combined. Add dressing to large bowl; toss gently to combine. Season to taste.
4 Arrange salad on a large serving platter. Top with labne and herbs; sprinkle with remaining za'atar.

prep time 10 minutes **serves** 6
nutritional count per serving 13.9g total fat (4.1g saturated fat); 715kJ (170 cal); 6.6g carbohydrate; 3g protein; 3.6g fibre
serving suggestion Crusty bread.

baby rocket, strawberry and walnut salad

melon, cucumber and white onion salad

baby rocket, strawberry and walnut salad

¾ cup (75g) walnuts

100g (3 ounces) baby rocket (arugula) leaves

500g (1 pound) small strawberries, halved

¼ cup (60ml) olive oil

1 cup (80g) shaved parmesan

¼ cup (60ml) strawberry-infused balsamic glaze

1 Stir nuts in a small frying pan over medium heat until toasted lightly. Cool; chop coarsely.
2 Place nuts in a large bowl with rocket, strawberries, oil and half the parmesan, season to taste; toss gently to combine.
3 Transfer salad to a serving bowl; sprinkle with remaining cheese and drizzle with balsamic glaze.

prep + cook time 15 minutes **serves** 4
nutritional count per serving 32.5g total fat (6.7g saturated fat); 1589kJ (380 cal); 7.9g carbohydrate; 12g protein; 3.3g fibre
tip If you can't find strawberry-infused balsamic glaze, use raspberry-infused or plain balsamic glaze.

melon, cucumber and white onion salad

1 medium rockmelon (cantaloupe) (1.7kg)

1 telegraph (hothouse) cucumber (400g), peeled

1 small white onion (80g)

1 cup (120g) pecans

200g (6½ ounces) fetta, crumbled

dressing

½ cup (125ml) olive oil

1 tablespoon grated lime rind

¼ cup (60ml) lime juice

1 tablespoon caster (superfine) sugar

1 Peel and seed melon, cut into large pieces. Using a vegetable peeler, peel ribbons from outside of cucumber until there are only seeds left; discard seeds. Using a mandoline or V-slicer, thinly slice onion into rings.
2 Stir nuts in a small frying pan over medium heat until toasted lightly. Cool; chop coarsely.
3 Make dressing.
4 Place melon, cucumber, onion, nuts and dressing in a large bowl; toss gently to combine. Top with fetta.
dressing Stir ingredients in a small bowl until sugar dissolves.

prep + cook time 25 minutes **serves** 6
nutritional count per serving 41.2g total fat (8.9g saturated fat); 2015kJ (481 cal); 16.6g carbohydrate; 9.5g protein; 4.9g fibre
tip You will need about 3 limes for this recipe.

moroccan pumpkin and chickpea salad

- ½ medium butternut pumpkin (1.4kg), peeled
- 2 tablespoons extra virgin olive oil
- 2 teaspoons ras el hanout
- 400g (12½ ounces) canned chickpeas (garbanzo beans), drained, rinsed
- 1 tablespoon lemon juice
- 1 tablespoon finely chopped preserved lemon rind
- 200g (6½ ounces) Greek-style yoghurt
- ½ small red onion (50g), sliced thinly
- 1 fresh long red chilli, chopped finely
- ½ cup loosely packed fresh coriander (cilantro) leaves
- ½ cup loosely packed fresh mint leaves

1 Preheat oven to 200°C/400°F.

2 Cut pumpkin into 2cm (¾-inch) thick wedges; place on a large baking-paper-lined oven tray. Combine oil and ras el hanout in a small bowl; brush over pumpkin. Season. Roast 20 minutes or until tender. Cool slightly.

3 Meanwhile, place a quarter of the chickpeas in a small bowl; mash with a fork. Stir in juice, rind and yoghurt; season to taste.

4 Arrange pumpkin on a serving platter; top with remaining chickpeas, onion and dressing. Sprinkle with chilli and herbs.

prep + cook time 30 minutes (+ cooling) **serves** 4

nutritional count per serving 14.2g total fat (3.5g saturated fat); 1530kJ (366 cal); 42.4g carbohydrate; 11.3g protein; 12.1g fibre

tip The salad and dressing can be made several hours ahead. Assemble salad close to serving.

vegetables

Showing off the delicious and diverse flavours of vegies, these recipes are perfect to serve as a main course, or side dish.

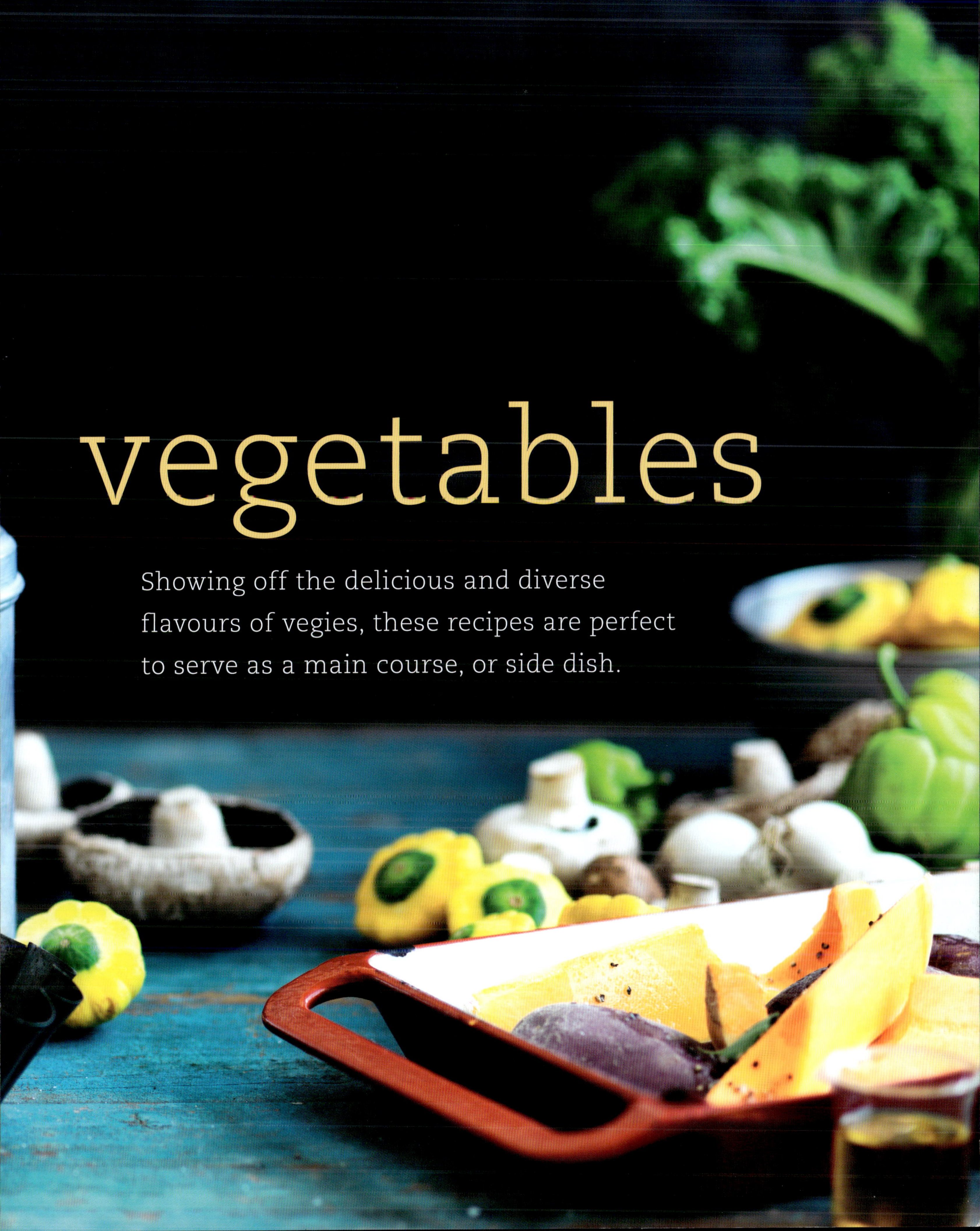

silver beet, ricotta and porcini fillo stacks

- 15g (½ ounce) dried porcini mushrooms
- ½ cup (80g) pine nuts
- 6 sheets fillo pastry
- olive oil spray
- ¾ cup (45g) finely grated parmesan
- 60g (2 ounces) butter
- 1 shallot (25g), chopped finely
- 150g (4½ ounces) oyster mushrooms
- 750g (1½ pounds) silver beet (swiss chard), trimmed, chopped coarsely
- 1 cup (240g) fresh ricotta
- 2 teaspoons finely grated lemon rind
- 2 tablespoons dried currants

1 Preheat oven to 180°C/350°F. Line two oven trays with baking paper.
2 Place porcini in a heatproof bowl; cover with boiling water.
3 Place half the pine nuts on another oven tray; roast 5 minutes or until fragrant. Place in a large bowl; cool.
4 Spray one sheet of pastry with oil; top with a second pastry sheet, spray with oil then top with a third sheet. Repeat to make two stacks. Cut each stack in half lengthways; cut each half into thirds to give 12 pieces. Place pastry pieces on lined trays. Coarsely chop remaining nuts; sprinkle nuts and ¼ cup of the parmesan on four of the pastry pieces.
5 Bake all pastry squares 8 minutes or until browned.
6 Meanwhile, heat butter in a large frying pan over medium-high heat; cook shallot, oyster and drained porcini mushrooms, stirring, until browned. Transfer to a large bowl with pine nuts.
7 Cook silver beet in same pan until wilted slightly. Transfer to the large bowl; stir in ricotta, rind, currants and remaining parmesan until just combined. Season to taste.
8 Place four of the plain pastry pieces on serving plates; top with half the silver beet mixture. Top each with another plain pastry piece, remaining silver beet mixture then pine nut pastry pieces. Serve immediately.

prep + cook time 25 minutes **makes** 4
nutritional count per stack 37.3g total fat (14.4g saturated fat); 2083kJ (498 cal); 22.1g carbohydrate; 17.7g protein; 3.9g fibre
tips Pastry pieces can be cooked a day ahead; reheat in the oven at 180°C/350°F about 5 minutes before assembling. The filling is best made just before serving.
serving suggestion Cherry tomato salad.

corn and kidney bean quesadillas with tomato salsa

3 large trimmed corn cobs (750g)

420g (13½ ounces) canned kidney beans, drained, rinsed

2 tablespoons coarsely chopped fresh coriander (cilantro)

⅔ cup (130g) pepitas (pumpkin seed kernels)

1½ cups (180g) grated cheddar

160g (5 ounces) fetta, crumbled

10 x 20cm (8-inch) flour tortillas

2 tablespoons extra virgin olive oil

1 cup (240g) sour cream

tomato salsa

2 medium roma (egg) tomatoes (300g)

2 tablespoons finely chopped pickled jalapeño chillies

½ small red onion (50g), chopped finely

1 tablespoon lime juice

1 tablespoon extra virgin olive oil

1 tablespoon coarsely chopped fresh coriander (cilantro)

1 Preheat a grill pan over medium heat. Cook corn, turning, 15 minutes or until tender and lightly charred. Cool slightly; cut kernels from cobs. Transfer to a medium bowl.

2 Meanwhile, make tomato salsa.

3 Preheat oven to 220°C/425°F.

4 Mash beans in a medium bowl to crush slightly. Stir in coriander, corn, half the pepitas, half the cheddar and half the fetta; season with black pepper.

5 Divide filling between tortillas, placing it over half of each tortilla, leaving a 1cm (½-inch) border. Fold tortillas over to enclose filling, pressing down firmly. Place on baking-paper-lined oven trays. Brush tops with oil. Scatter with combined remaining cheeses and pepitas.

6 Bake quesadillas 15 minutes, swapping trays from top to bottom, for even browning, or until browned lightly and filling is hot. Serve with salsa and sour cream.

tomato salsa Quarter tomatoes. Squeeze out seeds; finely chop. Combine tomato with remaining ingredients in a small bowl; season to taste.

prep + cook time 25 minutes **makes** 10

nutritional count per quesadilla 33.1g total fat (14.9g saturated fat); 1973kJ (471 cal); 24.9g carbohydrate; 17.3g protein; 6g fibre

tips You can substitute either 1 fresh red bird's-eye chilli or ½ teaspoon chilli flakes for pickled jalapeño if you like.
For a lower fat version, use reduced-fat cheeses and sour cream.

mushy fresh peas with almonds and artichokes

- ⅓ cup (45g) slivered almonds
- 1kg (2 pounds) fresh peas in pod, shelled
- 30g (1 ounce) butter
- 1 small leek (200g), trimmed, chopped finely
- 2 tablespoons fresh mint leaves
- 1 tablespoon sour cream
- 540g (1 pound) bottled artichoke hearts, drained
- ⅔ cup (160ml) pouring cream
- 1 tablespoon finely grated lemon rind
- 2 teaspoons lemon juice
- 60g (2 ounces) soft goat's cheese, crumbled
- ¼ cup loosely packed fresh mint leaves, extra

1 Stir nuts in a medium frying pan over low heat until toasted lightly. Cool.

2 Bring a medium saucepan of water to the boil over high heat. Add peas, return to the boil; drain immediately. Rinse under cold water until cooled.

3 Heat half the butter in a medium saucepan over medium heat; cook leek, stirring, until soft. Remove from heat; stir in peas. Add mint and sour cream; season to taste. Blend with a hand-held blender until just mushy. Cover to keep warm.

4 Heat remaining butter in a large frying pan over high heat; cook artichokes until browned lightly.

5 Heat cream, rind and juice in a medium saucepan over low heat until just warm. Add artichokes; stir to coat.

6 Divide pea mixture between four serving plates; top with artichokes. Sprinkle with nuts, cheese and extra mint.

prep + cook time 35 minutes **serves** 4
nutritional count per serving 32.4g total fat (17g saturated fat); 1745kJ (417 cal); 10.4g carbohydrate; 14.4g protein; 15.5g fibre
tip Replace fresh peas with 2½ cups (300g) frozen peas if you like.

roast cumin pumpkin and parsnip with hummus dressing

500g (1 pound) jap pumpkin

4 small parsnips (320g), halved lengthways

¼ cup (60ml) olive oil

1 tablespoon cumin seeds

2 teaspoons ground coriander

800g (1½ pounds) canned chickpeas (garbanzo beans), drained, rinsed

200g (6½ ounces) sourdough bread, torn into small chunks

¼ cup (60ml) olive oil, extra

½ cup loosely packed fresh flat-leaf parsley leaves, torn

½ cup loosely packed fresh mint leaves, torn

hummus dressing

1 tablespoon tahini

½ cup (120g) sour cream

2 tablespoons lemon juice

¼ teaspoon paprika

pinch cayenne pepper

¼ cup (60ml) cold water

1 Preheat oven to 220°C/425°F.

2 Cut unpeeled pumpkin into wedges. Place pumpkin and parsnips in a large bowl with oil and spices; season. Toss to combine. Place vegetables, in a single layer, on two baking-paper-lined oven trays; reserve spiced oil in the bowl. Roast vegetables 30 minutes, turning once during cooking.

3 Meanwhile, stir ¾ cup of the chickpeas into reserved spiced oil until coated; reserve.

4 Make hummus dressing.

5 Toss bread on an oven tray with extra oil until evenly coated; season. Cook bread on separate shelf in oven 8 minutes, stirring occasionally, or until bread is browned and crisp.

6 Add reserved chickpea mixture to vegetables; roast further 10 minutes or until vegetables are tender. Place vegetables and chickpeas on a serving platter with bread; drizzle with dressing and scatter with herbs.

hummus dressing Blend remaining 2 cups chickpeas with dressing ingredients until smooth. Season to taste.

prep + cook time 50 minutes **serves** 6

nutritional count per serving 31.5g total fat (8.4g saturated fat); 2147kJ (513 cal); 41g carbohydrate; 12.3g protein; 10g fibre

portobello bruschetta with grilled capsicum sauce

- 1 large red capsicum (bell pepper) (300g)
- 10g (½ ounce) butter
- 1 small leek (200g), chopped finely
- ¼ cup (60ml) pouring cream
- 4 x 2cm (¾-inch) thick slices crusty wholemeal bread
- 20g (¾ ounce) butter, extra
- 300g (9½ ounces) portobello mushrooms, sliced thickly
- ¼ teaspoon chilli flakes
- 1 teaspoon fennel seeds
- 2 teaspoons red wine vinegar
- ½ cup lightly packed fresh flat-leaf parsley leaves

1 Preheat grill (broiler) to high.
2 Quarter capsicum; discard seeds and membranes. Spray skin with cooking oil. Place capsicum under the grill, skin-side up, 8 minutes or until skin blisters and blackens. Cover capsicum pieces with plastic or paper for 10 minutes. Peel away skin; slice thickly.
3 Meanwhile, heat butter in a small saucepan over medium heat; cook leek, stirring, 5 minutes or until soft.
4 Blend capsicum, leek mixture and cream until smooth; season to taste.
5 Heat a grill plate (or grill or barbecue). Spray bread on both sides with cooking oil. Grill bread until toasted on both sides.
6 Heat extra butter in a large frying pan over medium heat; cook mushrooms, chilli and seeds, stirring occasionally, 5 minutes or until mushrooms are browned and slightly softened. Stir in vinegar; season to taste.
7 Spoon mushrooms onto toasted bread; drizzle each piece with about 1 tablespoon of capsicum sauce. Top with parsley.

prep + cook time 35 minutes **makes** 4
nutritional count per bruschetta 13.2g total fat (7.6g saturated fat); 1100kJ (263 cal); 22.7g carbohydrate; 10.2g protein; 7g fibre

steamed vegetables with curry dressing

500g (1 pound) jap pumpkin, unpeeled
2 medium eggplant (600g)
200g (6½ ounces) snow peas, trimmed
180g (5½ ounces) broccolini, halved lengthways
⅓ cup (15g) moist coconut flakes

curry dressing

3 fresh kaffir lime leaves
1 fresh long green chilli, chopped coarsely
1 teaspoon finely chopped fresh coriander (cilantro) root
1½ teaspoons finely grated lime rind
2cm (¾-inch) piece fresh ginger (10g), grated finely
1 clove garlic, peeled
½ teaspoon brown mustard seeds
¾ cup firmly packed fresh coriander (cilantro) leaves
1 teaspoon caster (superfine) sugar
¼ teaspoon salt
1 cup (250ml) coconut cream

1 Make curry dressing.
2 Cut pumpkin into wedges, leaving skin on. Cut eggplant into 3cm (1¼-inch) thick rounds. Steam pumpkin and eggplant, separately, in a large steamer over a large wok of simmering water 10 minutes or until vegetables are tender. Remove from steamer; cover to keep warm.
3 Steam snow peas and broccolini in same steamer 5 minutes or just until bright green.
4 Meanwhile, stir coconut flakes in a small frying pan over medium heat until toasted lightly.
5 Heat dressing in a small saucepan over low heat until warm.
6 Divide vegetables among serving plates; drizzle with dressing, sprinkle with coconut.
curry dressing Remove stem from lime leaves. Pound leaves with remaining ingredients, except coconut cream, in a mortar and pestle until it forms a paste. (Or, blend until a paste.) Stir in coconut cream until combined. Season to taste.

prep + cook time 35 minutes **serves** 4
nutritional count per serving 14.1g total fat (11.7g saturated fat); 1070kJ (255 cal); 19.7g carbohydrate; 7.8g protein; 10.9g fibre
serving suggestion Steamed jasmine rice.

kumara rösti with portobello mushrooms

- 1 large kumara (orange sweet potato) (500g)
- ½ cup (35g) panko (japanese) breadcrumbs
- 1 cup (80g) grated parmesan
- 2 eggs
- 2 cloves garlic, crushed
- ¼ cup (60ml) olive oil
- 80g (2½ ounces) butter, chopped
- ⅓ cup lightly packed fresh flat-leaf parsley leaves, chopped finely
- 2 teaspoons fresh thyme leaves, chopped finely
- 2 tablespoons finely chopped fresh chives
- 6 portobello mushrooms (480g)
- 150g (4½ ounces) baby spinach leaves
- ¼ cup (20g) shaved parmesan
- 1 medium lemon (140g), cut into wedges

1 Coarsely grate kumara; squeeze out excess liquid. Combine kumara with breadcrumbs, grated parmesan, egg, half the garlic and 1 tablespoon of the oil in a large bowl; season.

2 Line a 24cm (9½-inch) non-stick frying pan with baking paper. Add kumara mixture, pressing down firmly and evenly to cover base of pan; cook, covered, over medium heat 10 minutes or until browned underneath and kumara is almost tender. Slide rösti onto a flat plate; invert pan over rösti then turn pan and rösti over. Cook further 8 minutes or until rösti is browned underneath and cooked through.

3 Meanwhile, preheat oiled grill pan (or barbecue).

4 Stir butter, herbs and remaining garlic in a small saucepan, over low heat, until just melted.

5 Peel mushrooms; trim stalks to 1cm (½-inch). Brush a little of the butter mixture on both sides of mushrooms; season. Cook mushrooms in grill pan, 2 minutes each side or until browned and tender.

6 Cut rösti into wedges and divide between plates; top with spinach and mushrooms, then drizzle with remaining butter mixture. Top with shaved parmesan; serve with lemon wedges.

prep + cook time 35 minutes **serves** 4

nutritional count per serving 40.6g total fat (18.3g saturated fat); 2320kJ (554 cal); 23.6g carbohydrate; 21.3g protein; 5.7g fibre

tips Kumara turns brown when cut so it's best to grate it just before you use it.

If you have a scratch-free non-stick pan, you won't need to line it with baking paper.

roasted baby parsnips, fennel and potatoes

roasted asparagus and smashed potatoes

roasted baby parsnips, fennel and potatoes

2 baby fennel bulbs (260g)

6 small parsnips (720g), halved lengthways

6 baby new potatoes (240g), halved

6 cloves garlic, unpeeled

2 star anise

2 tablespoons olive oil

2 teaspoons cumin seeds

¼ cup (40g) seeded kalamata olives, chopped coarsely

dressing

2 tablespoons finely chopped fresh flat-leaf parsley

¼ cup (60ml) olive oil

1½ tablespoons lemon juice

2 teaspoons dijon mustard

1 Preheat oven to 200°C/400°F.
2 Trim fennel, reserve fronds. Cut fennel into eight wedges.
3 Place fennel, parsnip, potato, garlic and star anise in a large baking dish. Drizzle with oil, sprinkle with cumin; season. Roast vegetables 30 minutes or until potatoes are tender.
4 Meanwhile, make dressing.
5 Sprinkle vegetables with olives and reserved fennel fronds; drizzle with dressing.
dressing Place ingredients in a screw-top jar; shake well. Season to taste.

prep + cook time 35 minutes **serves** 4
nutritional count per serving 25.6g total fat (3.9g saturated fat); 1568kJ (375 cal); 26.4g carbohydrate; 5.6g protein; 8.8g fibre
tip Pumpkin, kumara, zucchini and eggplant would all be suitable to use in place of some of the vegetables in this recipe.
serving suggestion Fried or barbecued haloumi and crusty bread, for a main meal.

roasted asparagus and smashed potatoes

700g (1½ ounces) baby new potatoes

¼ cup (60ml) macadamia oil

340g (11 ounces) green asparagus, trimmed

340g (11 ounces) white asparagus, trimmed

¾ cup (100g) macadamias, chopped coarsely

100g (3 ounces) shaved parmesan

1 Preheat oven to 220°C/425°F.
2 Boil, steam or microwave potatoes until just tender; drain. Press warm potatoes lightly inside a tea towel with the palm of your hand. Place potatoes in a large shallow baking-paper-lined baking dish; season. Drizzle half the oil over potatoes.
3 Roast potatoes 20 minutes.
4 Place asparagus on potatoes; drizzle with remaining oil, sprinkle with nuts. Roast in oven for further 5 minutes or until the edges of the potatoes are crisp and golden and asparagus is tender.
5 Serve asparagus and potatoes sprinkled with cheese.

prep + cook time 45 minutes **serves** 4
nutritional count per serving 40.5g total fat (9.1g saturated fat); 2278kJ (545 cal); 24.3g carbohydrate; 17.5g protein; 5.6g fibre
tip If white asparagus is unavailable, use all green asparagus or thin baby carrots instead.

mexican stuffed potatoes with spiced tomato and avocado salsa

- 4 large potatoes (1.2kg)
- 1 tablespoon olive oil
- 1 small red onion (100g), chopped finely
- 2 cloves garlic, crushed
- 30g (1 ounce) packaged burrito spice mix
- 400g (12½ ounces) canned red kidney beans, drained, rinsed
- 400g (12½ ounces) canned crushed tomatoes
- 1 cup (250ml) water
- ½ cup (120g) sour cream
- ½ cup loosely packed fresh coriander (cilantro) leaves

spiced tomato and avocado salsa

- 1 large tomato (220g), cut into 1cm (½-inch) pieces
- 1 medium avocado (250g), cut into 1cm (½-inch) pieces
- 2 tablespoons lime juice
- ¼ cup lightly packed fresh coriander (cilantro) leaves, chopped finely
- 2 tablespoons olive oil
- 2 teaspoons Tabasco

1 Scrub potatoes well. Prick skin all over with a fork. Cook in microwave oven on HIGH (100%) 10 minutes or until tender when pierced with a skewer. Cover to keep warm.

2 Heat oil in a large saucepan; cook onion and garlic, stirring, 3 minutes or until onion begins to soften. Stir in spice mix and beans, then tomatoes and the water; bring to the boil. Reduce heat; simmer, uncovered, 10 minutes or until thickened slightly. Season to taste.

3 Meanwhile, make spiced avocado and tomato salsa.

4 Cut a cross, about 5cm (2 inches) deep, in the top of each potato. Press on the sides of the potato until the cross opens up to form a cavity; place on serving plates.

5 Spoon bean mixture onto potatoes; top with sour cream, salsa and coriander.

spiced tomato and avocado salsa Combine ingredients in a medium bowl; season to taste.

prep + cook time 40 minutes **serves** 4

nutritional count per serving 35.8g total fat (11.8g saturated fat); 2685kJ (641 cal); 56.2g carbohydrate; 15.7g protein; 13.5g fibre

tips Potato cooking time will depend on the wattage of your microwave.

If you don't like too much chilli heat, start by adding a dash of Tabasco to the salsa, then increase to taste.

serving suggestion Rocket (arugula) leaves or a green salad and lime wedges.

roasted beetroot with goat's cheese and walnuts

- 1kg (2 pounds) baby beetroot (beets)
- 1 tablespoon extra virgin olive oil
- 120g (4 ounces) baby salad leaves (or mesclun)
- ½ cup (50g) roasted whole walnuts
- 150g (4½ ounces) ashed goat's cheese log

red wine vinegar dressing

- ⅓ cup (80ml) light olive oil
- 1 tablespoon extra virgin olive oil
- 2 tablespoons red wine vinegar
- 1 teaspoon caster (superfine) sugar
- 1 small clove garlic, crushed
- 1 teaspoon coarsely chopped fresh thyme

1 Preheat oven to 200°C/400°F.
2 Wash beetroot well. Trim beetroot, leaving 4cm (1½-inch) stem attached. Halve or quarter larger beetroot. Place beetroot in a shallow baking dish; drizzle with oil, season. Roast 30 minutes or until tender. Cool slightly; rub off skins.
3 Meanwhile, make red wine vinegar dressing.
4 Place warm beetroot in a shallow serving bowl with leaves and nuts, season; toss gently to combine. Crumble cheese over salad, drizzle with dressing.
red wine vinegar dressing Place ingredients in a screw-top jar; shake well.

prep + cook time 40 minutes **serves** 4
nutritional count per serving 44.1g total fat (10.2g saturated fat); 2240kJ (535 cal); 19.2g carbohydrate; 12.7g protein; 9.1g fibre
tip You can use baby spinach leaves or your favourite lettuce leaves instead of the baby salad leaves, if you like.

warm green salad with soft eggs and hazelnut dressing

- 270g (8½ ounces) brussels sprouts
- 500g (1 pound) baby new potatoes, quartered
- 170g (5½ ounces) asparagus, halved lengthways
- 150g (5 ounces) fresh peas in pod, shelled
- 4 eggs, refrigerated
- 1 tablespoon olive oil
- ½ cup (70g) roasted hazelnuts, chopped coarsely
- 60g (2 ounces) goat's cheese, crumbled
- ¼ cup loosely packed fresh chervil leaves

hazelnut dressing

- ¼ cup (60ml) lemon juice
- 2 tablespoons hazelnut oil
- 1 tablespoon olive oil
- ⅓ cup loosely packed fresh chervil, chopped coarsely

1 Discard outer leaves from brussels sprouts; cut sprouts into quarters.
2 Make hazelnut dressing.
3 Place potato in a medium saucepan, cover with cold water; bring to the boil. Boil, uncovered, 12 minutes or until tender. In the last minute of cooking time, add asparagus and peas. Drain vegetables; transfer to a medium bowl. Add 1 tablespoon of the dressing. Season to taste.
4 Meanwhile, cover eggs with cold water in a small saucepan; bring to the boil. Boil, uncovered, 3 minutes. Drain; rinse eggs under cold water until cool enough to handle. Peel immediately.
5 Heat oil in a large frying pan over medium heat; cook brussels sprouts, stirring, until browned lightly and crisp.
6 Arrange vegetables on a large serving platter. Tear eggs in half, place on vegetables. Sprinkle with nuts and cheese. Drizzle with remaining dressing, sprinkle with chervil leaves.
hazelnut dressing Place ingredients in a screw-top jar; shake well. Season to taste.

prep + cook time 35 minutes **serves** 4
nutritional count per serving 37.9g total fat (7.3g saturated fat); 2167kJ (518 cal); 20.4g carbohydrate; 20g protein; 8.8g fibre
tip Replace fresh peas with ½ cup (60g) frozen peas if you like.

No 4

cheese
eggs &

Full of calcium to ensure healthy teeth and bones, these wonderful recipes are ideal for breakfast, lunch and dinner.

ricotta and basil pancakes with tomato and rocket salad

- 300g (9½ ounces) baby truss roma (egg) tomatoes
- 2 tablespoons extra virgin olive oil
- 1 cup (240g) ricotta
- 1 egg
- 1¼ cups (310ml) milk
- 1¼ cups (185g) self-raising flour
- ½ cup coarsely chopped fresh basil
- ¼ cup (20g) grated parmesan
- 30g (1 ounce) butter
- 1 tablespoon white balsamic vinegar
- 250g (8 ounces) rocket (arugula)
- ½ small red onion (50g), sliced thinly

1 Preheat oven to 220°C/425°F. Place tomatoes in a small baking dish; drizzle with half the oil. Season. Roast 10 minutes or until skins just split.
2 Whisk ricotta and egg in a medium bowl until combined. Whisk in milk, then flour. Stir in basil and parmesan; season.
3 Melt a little of the butter in a large non-stick frying pan over medium heat. Pour ¼-cups of mixture into pan, allowing room for spreading. Cook pancakes 2 minutes each side or until golden and cooked through. Stack pancakes; cover to keep warm. Wipe out pan with absorbent paper; repeat with remaining butter and batter to make 12 pancakes in total.
4 Drizzle remaining oil and vinegar over rocket and onion in a medium bowl, season to taste; toss gently to combine.
5 Serve warm pancakes topped with rocket mixture, tomatoes and any remaining dressing.

prep + cook time 45 minutes **serves** 4
nutritional count per serving 21.7g total fat (11g saturated fat); 1920kJ (459 cal); 44.5g carbohydrate; 19.2g protein; 4.1g fibre
tip Wipe the pan clean with absorbent paper between each batch of pancakes so they don't over-brown.

zucchini tarts

turkish eggs

zucchini tarts

2 sheets puff pastry

½ cup (125g) mascarpone cheese

2 eggs

½ cup (40g) grated parmesan

340g (11 ounces) baby zucchini, sliced thinly lengthways

1 Preheat oven to 220°C/425°F. Line two oven trays with baking paper.

2 Cut pastry sheets in half; place two halves on each tray about 5cm (2 inches) apart. With the back of a small knife, mark a 1cm (½-inch) border on pastry pieces. Prick bases inside border with a fork.

3 Bake pastry 10 minutes or until golden. Using a clean tea towel, press down carefully on the centre of each tart.

4 Meanwhile, combine mascarpone, egg and 1 tablespoon of the parmesan in a medium bowl; season well.

5 Spread egg mixture over tart bases; top with zucchini slices, slightly overlapping. Sprinkle with remaining parmesan.

6 Bake tarts 12 minutes or until golden.

prep + cook time 40 minutes **makes** 4

nutritional count per tart 38.8g total fat (22.5g saturated fat); 2395kJ (572 cal); 40.9g carbohydrate; 14.4g protein; 2.4g fibre

tip Use a mandoline or V-slicer to slice the zucchini quickly and evenly.

serving suggestion Tomato and basil salad.

turkish eggs

1½ tablespoons olive oil

1 large brown onion (200g), sliced thinly

1 large red capsicum (bell pepper) (350g), sliced thinly

400g (12½ ounces) canned diced tomatoes

¼ teaspoon dried chilli flakes

¼ teaspoon sweet paprika

1 cup (280g) Greek-style yoghurt

1 clove garlic, crushed

4 eggs

1 Heat oil in a large frying pan over medium-high heat; cook onion and capsicum, stirring, 10 minutes or until softened and well browned. Stir in tomatoes, chilli and paprika; season to taste.

2 Combine yoghurt and garlic in a small bowl; season to taste.

3 Make four small indents in capsicum mixture with the back of a spoon. Break one egg into a cup; slide egg into an indent. Repeat with remaining eggs. Cook, covered, over medium heat 6 minutes or until egg whites are set.

4 Serve with garlic yoghurt.

prep + cook time 25 minutes **serves** 4

nutritional count per serving 16.7g total fat (5.7g saturated fat); 1184kJ (283 cal); 17.5g carbohydrate; 13.7g protein; 3.8g fibre

tip You can serve the dish topped with crumbled persian fetta instead of the yoghurt mixture.

serving suggestion Toasted turkish bread.

seared haloumi with zucchini and basil

- ⅔ cup (90g) slivered almonds
- 2 medium zucchini (240g)
- 1 tablespoon finely grated lemon rind
- 1 tablespoon lemon juice
- 1 cup firmly packed fresh basil leaves
- 1 fresh small red chilli
- ⅔ cup (160ml) olive oil
- 2 x 180g (5½-ounce) packets haloumi cheese
- 1 tablespoon olive oil, extra
- 1 medium lemon (140g), cut into wedges

1 Stir nuts in a large frying pan over medium heat until toasted lightly. Remove from pan. Cool. Reserve 2 tablespoons.
2 Meanwhile, using a vegetable peeler, cut ribbons lengthways from zucchini.
3 Blend rind, juice, basil, chilli, nuts and half the oil until chopped finely. Transfer mixture to a small bowl; stir in remaining oil. Season to taste.
4 Just before serving, cut each block of haloumi in half horizontally then cut each half into three pieces crossways. Heat extra oil in same pan over medium heat; cook haloumi over low heat until browned on both sides.
5 Layer haloumi and zucchini on serving plates. Drizzle with basil mixture then sprinkle with reserved nuts. Serve with lemon wedges.

prep + cook time 20 minutes **serves** 4
nutritional count per serving 69.1g total fat (17.3g saturated fat); 3088kJ (739 cal); 4.3g carbohydrate; 24.6g protein; 3.8g fibre
tips The basil mixture, without the lemon rind and juice, can be made several days ahead; keep tightly covered in the refrigerator or freeze for up to 3 months. Add the lemon just before serving.
Make sure you cook the haloumi just before serving, as it becomes tough and rubbery on cooling.
serving suggestion Grilled flat bread.

individual egg, spinach and tomato bread cases

- 1 cob loaf (450g)
- 30g (1 ounce) baby spinach leaves
- 8 eggs
- 4 small heirloom tomatoes (120g), halved
- 100g (3 ounces) ricotta
- ⅓ cup loosely packed fresh basil leaves

1 Preheat oven to 180°C/350°F. Spray four 13cm (5¼-inch) individual pie tins with olive oil spray. Place on an oven tray.
2 Cut four 1.5cm (¾-inch) thick slices crossways from bread. Trim crusts from bread slices. Roll bread gently with rolling pin to flatten slightly. Line tins with bread slices; trim bread with kitchen scissors.
3 Bake bread cases 10 minutes or until bread is dried out but not coloured.
4 Divide spinach leaves between bread cases; crack two eggs into each case, top with tomatoes. Drop small spoonfuls of cheese into cases. Season.
5 Bake cases further 15 minutes or until the egg whites are set. Sprinkle with basil.

prep + cook time 40 minutes **makes** 4
nutritional count per case 14.6g total fat (5.3g saturated fat); 15.4kJ (360 cal); 32g carbohydrate; 23.6g protein; 3.2g fibre
tips You can use halved cherry, grape or mini roma (egg) tomatoes if you like.
This recipe would make a delicious breakfast or brunch dish.
serving suggestion Green salad or steamed asparagus.

tomato, mozzarella and chickpea pan bake

- ½ loaf ciabatta (300g), crusts removed, torn into 2cm (¾-inch) pieces
- 400g (12½ ounces) grape tomatoes, halved lengthways
- ⅓ cup (80ml) extra virgin olive oil
- 400g (12½ ounces) canned chickpeas (garbanzo beans), drained, rinsed
- 100g (3 ounces) fresh ricotta
- 10 eggs
- 2 cloves garlic, crushed
- ¾ cup coarsely chopped fresh flat-leaf parsley
- ½ cup (40g) finely grated parmesan
- 1 tablespoon drained baby capers
- ⅔ cup (100g) pitted kalamata olives, halved
- 1 ball buffalo mozzarella (110g), torn
- 2 tablespoons fresh basil leaves, torn

1 Preheat oven to 220°C/425°F.
2 Place bread on a baking-paper-lined oven tray. Squeeze seeds and juices from tomatoes over bread; place tomatoes on tray. Drizzle with half the oil; season to taste. Roast 15 minutes, stirring occasionally or until bread is golden and tomatoes soft.
3 Meanwhile, using a potato masher, lightly crush chickpeas in a large bowl; season. Whisk in ricotta, eggs, garlic, parsley and three quarters of the parmesan until combined. Stir in capers, olives and half the tomato mixture. Season.
4 Heat remaining oil in an ovenproof 26cm (10½-inch) heavy-based frying pan over medium heat until very hot. Immediately add egg mixture; top with remaining tomato mixture and parmesan. Cook 8 minutes or until browned around the edge and half set.
5 Cover loosely with baking paper; bake in the oven 15 minutes or until set. Stand bake 5 minutes. Invert onto a large plate; flip onto a second large plate right-way up. Serve topped with mozzarella and basil. Drizzle with a little extra oil, if you like.

prep + cook time 1 hour **serves** 6
nutritional count per serving 34.4g total fat (10.7g saturated fat); 2355kJ (563 cal); 32g carbohydrate; 28.6g protein; 5.8g fibre
tip Buffalo mozzarella has a more tangy lactic dairy taste than cow's milk mozzarella. You can use bocconcini instead, if you prefer.

new curried egg salad

- 8 eggs
- 1 teaspoon yellow mustard seeds
- ¼ teaspoon cumin seeds
- ¼ teaspoon ground turmeric
- ¼ teaspoon ground coriander
- ¼ cup (60ml) vegetable oil
- 2 fresh long red chillies, sliced thinly
- 8 curry leaves
- ⅔ cup (190g) thick Greek-style yoghurt
- 1 tablespoon lemon juice
- 2 green onions (scallions), chopped finely
- 100g (3 ounces) baby spinach leaves
- 8 mini pappadums (30g)

1 Cover eggs with cold water in a medium saucepan. Bring to the boil over a high heat. Boil, uncovered, 3 minutes. Drain; rinse eggs under cold water until cool enough to handle. Immediately peel eggs.
2 Meanwhile, dry fry seeds and spices in a small frying pan over medium heat 2 minutes or until fragrant; transfer to a medium bowl.
3 Heat oil in same pan; cook chilli, stirring, over medium heat 3 minutes or until softened. Remove from pan with a slotted spoon; drain on absorbent paper. Add curry leaves to same pan; cook until bright green. Drain on absorbent paper.
4 Stir yoghurt, juice and onion into spice mixture; season to taste.
5 Arrange spinach, torn eggs and broken pappadums on plates. Drizzle with yoghurt mixture; sprinkle with chilli and curry leaves.

prep + cook time 20 minutes **serves** 4
nutritional count per serving 29.4g total fat (8.1g saturated fat); 1634kJ (390 cal); 11.9g carbohydrate; 19.7g protein; 1.6g fibre
tip You can leave the chilli out if you like.

potato, spinach and goat's cheese soufflés

- 1 medium potato (200g), cut into 1cm (½-inch) cubes
- 100g (3 ounces) baby spinach leaves
- ¼ cup (60ml) pouring cream
- 2 teaspoons wholegrain mustard
- 75g (2½ ounces) goat's cheese, crumbled
- ¼ cup (20g) finely grated parmesan
- 2 eggs, separated
- 1½ tabelspoons finely chopped fresh chives
- 1 large green cucumber (400g), peeled, chopped finely
- ½ cup lightly packed fresh mint leaves, chopped coarsely
- 1 tablespoon lemon juice
- 1 tablespoon extra virgin olive oil

1 Preheat oven to 220°C/425°F. Oil four 1-cup (250ml) ramekins; place ramekins on an oven tray.

2 Boil, steam or microwave potato until cooked through.

3 Meanwhile, place spinach leaves in a medium bowl, cover with boiling water; drain. Refresh under cold water; drain. Squeeze excess water from spinach with absorbent paper; chop finely.

4 Combine potato and spinach in a medium bowl; season. Divide mixture between ramekins.

5 Stir cream, mustard and cheeses in a small saucepan over low heat until just warm. Pour mixture into a medium bowl; stir in egg yolks and chives. Season.

6 Beat egg whites in a small bowl with an electric mixer until soft peaks form. Gently fold egg white into cheese mixture. Spoon mixture into ramekins.

7 Bake soufflés 10 minutes or until puffed and browned.

8 Meanwhile, combine cucumber, mint, juice and oil in a small bowl; season to taste.

9 Serve soufflés immediately with cucumber salsa.

prep + cook time 30 minutes **serves** 4

nutritional count per serving 18.5g total fat (8.8g saturated fat); 1032kJ (247 cal); 7.7g carbohydrate; 11.6g protein; 2.2g fibre

tip This is a quick version of making a soufflé as the base is not made on a flour-thickened cheese sauce.

asian-style omelette with glass noodles

120g (4 ounces) bean thread noodles

2 tablespoons peanut or vegetable oil

2 cloves garlic, crushed

100g (3 ounces) shiitake mushrooms, sliced thinly

12 eggs

1½ cups (375ml) water

1 cup (350g) oyster-flavoured sauce

1 tablespoon cornflour (cornstarch)

2 green onions (scallions), sliced thinly

2 cups (160g) bean sprouts

1 fresh long red chilli, sliced thinly

1 cup loosely packed fresh coriander (cilantro) leaves

1 Place noodles in a large heatproof bowl; cover with boiling water. Stand 4 minutes or until noodles are tender; drain.
2 Meanwhile, heat half the oil in a medium frying pan over medium-high heat; cook garlic and mushrooms, stirring, 2 minutes or until mushrooms are tender. Season to taste. Transfer to a small bowl.
3 Lightly whisk eggs and ½ cup of the water in a large jug. Blend sauce, cornflour and remaining water in a small bowl until smooth.
4 Heat 1 teaspoon of the remaining oil in a medium non-stick frying pan over high heat; pour in a quarter of the egg mixture. Working quickly, sprinkle omelette with a quarter each of the onion, mushrooms and noodles. Using a large metal spatula, gently lift edges of omelette away from pan, swirl pan to move uncooked egg to the edge of pan. Lift the edges of the omelette away from pan, gently moving spatula under omelette. Fold omelette in half. Pour a quarter of the oyster sauce mixture into the pan; cook a further 1 minute or until sauce thickens. Remove omelette from pan. Rinse and wipe out pan.
5 Repeat with remaining ingredients to make four omelettes. Top omelettes with bean sprouts, chilli and coriander to serve.

prep + cook time 25 minutes **serves** 4
nutritional count per serving 26.4g total fat (7.5g saturated fat); 2344kJ (560 cal); 50.4g carbohydrate; 27.6g protein; 2.7g fibre
tips If you want to serve the omelettes at the same time, preheat the oven to 120°C/250°F before preparing this recipe to heat the serving plates and to keep the omelettes warm as you cook them.
Choose an oyster-flavoured sauce without any seafood content. Check the label if you are unsure.

grains & pulses

Make pulses and grains part of your regular diet to ensure you get sufficient amounts of iron, protein, calcium and zinc.

radicchio and pear risotto

- 1 litre (4 cups) vegetable stock
- 1 cup (250ml) water
- 1½ tablespoons olive oil
- 1 medium brown onion (150g), chopped finely
- 1½ cups (300g) arborio rice
- ½ cup (125ml) white wine
- 2 medium pears (460g)
- 50g (1½ ounces) butter
- 1 tablespoon balsamic glaze
- 1 medium radicchio (200g), trimmed, shredded coarsely
- 1 cup (80g) grated parmesan
- ½ cup loosely packed fresh flat-leaf parsley leaves

1 Bring stock and the water to the boil, over high heat, in a medium saucepan. Reduce heat to low; simmer, covered.

2 Meanwhile, heat oil in a large saucepan over medium heat; cook onion, stirring, until soft. Add rice; stir to coat in mixture. Add wine; cook, stirring, until liquid is almost evaporated.

3 Add 1 cup of the hot stock; cook, stirring gently, over medium heat until liquid is absorbed. Continue adding stock, in 1-cup batches, stirring until stock is absorbed after each addition. Total cooking time should be 20 minutes or until rice is tender.

4 Meanwhile, cut pears into six wedges each; remove cores. Heat half the butter in a large frying pan over medium heat; cook pear until tender and starting to caramelise. Add glaze; turn pears to coat. Remove from heat; cover to keep warm.

5 Remove risotto from heat; stir in remaining butter, radicchio and parmesan. Season to taste. Stand, covered, 1 minute. Serve risotto topped with pear and parsley; and, if you like, with shaved parmesan.

prep + cook time 45 minutes **serves** 4

nutritional count per serving 24.2g total fat (11.7g saturated fat); 2597kJ (620 cal); 78.4g carbohydrate; 15.6g protein; 6.7g fibre

tip Serve risotto quickly after stirring the radicchio through the rice, as the radicchio will discolour.

serving suggestion A green salad.

quinoa, zucchini and fetta salad

- ¾ cup (150g) white quinoa
- 1½ cups (375ml) water
- ½ cup (70g) hazelnuts
- 2 medium zucchini (240g), cut into long thin strips
- 250g (8 ounces) heirloom or mixed cherry tomatoes, halved
- ½ small red onion (50g), sliced thinly
- 100g (3 ounces) fetta, crumbled
- 1 cup loosely packed fresh small basil leaves
- 2 tablespoons extra virgin olive oil
- 1 tablespoon red wine vinegar

1 Rinse quinoa under cold water; drain well. Place in a medium saucepan with the water; bring to the boil. Reduce heat; simmer, covered, 15 minutes or until water is absorbed and quinoa is tender. Transfer to a large serving bowl to cool.

2 Meanwhile, roast hazelnuts in a medium frying pan over medium heat 4 minutes or until golden. Rub hot hazelnuts in a clean tea towel to remove most of the skin; discard skin. Coarsely chop nuts.

3 Add nuts to quinoa in bowl with zucchini, tomato, onion, half the fetta and half the basil. Drizzle with combined oil and vinegar; toss gently to combine. Season to taste. Serve topped with remaining fetta and basil.

prep + cook time 25 minutes (+ cooling) **serves** 4

nutritional count per serving 28.8g total fat (6g saturated fat); 1800kJ (430 cal); 25.7g carbohydrate; 13.5g protein; 6.5g fibre

tip You can use a mandoline or V-slicer for the zucchini or coarsely grate it, if you like.

serving suggestion A green salad or steamed asparagus and crusty bread.

roasted broccoli with barley and haloumi

1 cup (200g) pearl barley

850g (1¾ pounds) broccoli

3 cloves garlic, sliced thinly

2 fresh long red chillies, halved lengthways, seeded, sliced thinly

½ cup (125ml) extra virgin olive oil

180g (5½ ounces) haloumi cheese, cut into 1.5cm (¾-inch)-thick slices

2 tablespoons lemon juice

1 cup loosely packed torn fresh mint leaves

1 cup coarsely chopped fresh coriander (cilantro) leaves

2 tablespoons dukkah

1 Preheat oven to 220°C/425°F.
2 Cook barley in a large saucepan of boiling salted water, uncovered, 30 minutes or until tender; drain.
3 Meanwhile, cut broccoli into large florets. Combine broccoli, garlic, chilli and ¼ cup of the oil in a large shallow baking dish; season. Roast 10 minutes or until broccoli is almost tender and beginning to brown. Add haloumi; roast further 10 minutes or until haloumi is heated through and browned lightly.
4 Drizzle remaining oil and juice over broccoli mixture. Combine broccoli mixture with barley and herbs. Season to taste. Serve sprinkled with dukkah.

prep + cook time 35 minutes **serves** 4
nutritional count per serving 41.1g total fat (10.1g saturated fat); 2600kJ (621 cal); 34.3g carbohydrate; 22.4g protein; 13g fibre
tip This recipe would also be delicious using cauliflower instead of broccoli, or a mixture of both.

green barley salad

1 cup (200g) pearl barley

1 cup (120g) frozen peas

1 cup (150g) shelled edamame

150g (4½ ounces) snow peas, sliced thinly

2 green onions (scallions), chopped finely

½ cup loosely packed fresh mint leaves

2 tablespoons extra virgin olive oil

1 tablespoon lemon juice

335g (10½ ounces) labne in olive oil, drained

1 Cook barley in a medium saucepan of salted water over medium heat about 25 minutes or until tender. Drain; rinse under cold water until cold, drain well.
2 Meanwhile, bring a medium saucepan of salted water to the boil. Add peas, edamame and snow peas; boil 1 minute. Drain; place in a bowl of iced water until cold. Drain well.
3 Place barley and pea mixture in a shallow serving dish with onion and mint; drizzle with combined oil and juice. Toss gently to combine. Season to taste.
4 Serve salad topped with labne.

prep + cook time 30 minutes **serves** 6
nutritional count per serving 20.9g total fat (2.9g saturated fat); 1448kJ (346 cal); 28.6g carbohydrate; 9.3g protein; 6.4g fibre
tip Frozen edamame, soy beans in the pod, are available from Asian supermarkets. You will need about 300g (9½ ounces) in the pod. You can also use frozen broad (fava) beans; you'll need to discard the outer skin after the podded beans have been brought to the boil.

roasted broccoli with barley and haloumi

green barley salad

soft polenta with mixed mushrooms

- 2 cups (500ml) milk
- 2 cups (500ml) vegetable stock
- 1 cup (170g) instant polenta
- ½ cup (40g) grated parmesan
- 100g (3 ounces) butter, chopped
- 200g (6½ ounces) swiss brown mushrooms, sliced thinly
- 200g (6½ ounces) button mushrooms, sliced thinly
- 3 shallots (75g), chopped finely
- 1 fresh long red chilli, sliced thinly
- 100g (3 ounces) oyster mushrooms, halved
- 2 cloves garlic, crushed
- 100g (3 ounces) baby spinach leaves
- ½ cup (70g) roasted hazelnuts, chopped coarsely

1 Bring milk and stock to the boil in a large saucepan. Gradually add polenta, stirring; cook, stirring occasionally, over medium heat, 10 minutes or until polenta is thick and smooth. Stir in cheese and 40g (1½ ounces) of the butter until melted. Season to taste; cover to keep warm.

2 Meanwhile, heat remaining butter in a large frying pan over high heat; cook swiss brown and button mushrooms, shallot and chilli, stirring occasionally, until browned lightly. Add oyster mushrooms and garlic; cook, stirring, until softened. Add spinach and nuts; toss well. Season to taste.

3 Serve soft polenta topped with mushroom mixture.

prep + cook time 20 minutes **serves** 4

nutritional count per serving 40.6g total fat (14.3g saturated fat); 2620kJ (627 cal); 42.5g carbohydrate; 21g protein; 6.5g fibre

brown fried rice with carrot, cabbage and red onion

barley with pistachio and green olives

brown fried rice with carrot, cabbage and red onion

1⅓ cups (265g) medium-grain brown rice

1 tablespoon peanut oil

2 eggs, beaten lightly

3 small carrots (200g)

1 medium red onion (170g), cut into wedges

300g (9½ ounces) red cabbage, shredded coarsely

2 cloves garlic, crushed

4cm (1½-inch) piece fresh ginger (20g), grated

2 green onions (scallions), sliced thinly

1½ tablespoons light soy sauce

1 fresh long red chilli, sliced thinly

1 Cook rice in a medium saucepan of boiling salted water 35 minutes or until tender; drain. Rinse under cold water; drain well.
2 Meanwhile, heat a large wok on medium-high heat; add 1 teaspoon of the oil, swirl to coat wok. Add egg; swirl wok to make a thin omelette. Cook 30 seconds or until just set; slide omelette onto a clean board. Roll tightly; cut into strips.
3 Thinly slice carrots on the diagonal.
4 Heat remaining oil in same wok; stir fry carrot and red onion 4 minutes or until just tender. Add cabbage; stir-fry 2 minutes or until wilted. Add garlic, ginger and half the green onion; stir fry until fragrant. Add rice and sauce; stir fry until hot.
5 Serve fried rice topped with omelette strips, chilli and remaining green onion.

prep + cook time 40 minutes **serves** 4
nutritional count per serving 9.2g total fat (2.1g saturated fat); 1592kJ (380 cal); 57.9g carbohydrate; 11.9g protein; 8.1g fibre
tip Serve with extra soy sauce if you like.

barley with pistachio and green olives

1½ cup (300g) pearl barley

4 large pitta bread (320g)

¾ cup (210g) Greek-style yoghurt

1 teaspoon finely grated lemon rind

1 cup loosely packed fresh mint leaves, chopped finely

2 cups (280g) green (sicilian) olives

¾ cup (100g) shelled pistachios

¼ radicchio (80g), shredded finely

1 long green chilli, chopped finely

¼ cup (60ml) lemon juice

2 tablespoons olive oil

1 Cook barley in a medium saucepan of boiling water 20 minutes or until tender; drain.
2 Heat a grill plate (or grill or barbecue); cook bread until toasted lightly on both sides.
3 Meanwhile, combine yoghurt, rind and 2 teaspoons of the mint in a small bowl.
4 Place barley in a large bowl with olives, nuts, radicchio, chilli, juice, oil and remaining mint; toss gently to combine. Season to taste. Serve with toasted bread, minted yoghurt and, if you like, some extra mint leaves.

prep + cook time 30 minutes **serves** 4
nutritional count per serving 42.8g total fat (7.4g saturated fat); 3820kJ (913 cal); 99.9g carbohydrate; 23g protein; 16.7g fibre
tip Grate the rind from the lemon before you juice it.

cauliflower and rocket risotto

650g (1¼ pounds) cauliflower, cut into florets
1 tablespoon olive oil
1 teaspoon fresh thyme leaves
1 litre (4 cups) vegetable stock
2 cup (500ml) water
40g (1½ ounces) butter
1 medium brown onion (150g), chopped finely
2 cloves garlic, crushed
1½ cups (300g) arborio rice
⅓ cup (80ml) white wine
½ cup (40g) shaved parmesan
10g (½ ounce) butter, extra
2 tablespoons roasted pine nuts
125g (4 ounces) rocket (arugula), shredded coarsely

1 Preheat oven to 220°C/425°F.
2 Combine cauliflower, oil and thyme on an oven tray; season. Roast 15 minutes or until just tender and browned.
3 Meanwhile, bring stock and the water to the boil in a large saucepan. Reduce heat; simmer, covered.
4 Heat butter in a large saucepan over medium heat; cook onion and garlic, stirring, 5 minutes or until soft but not coloured. Add rice; stir to coat in onion mixture. Add wine; cook, stirring, until liquid has evaporated.
5 Add 1 cup of the hot stock mixture; cook, stirring gently, over medium heat until liquid is absorbed. Continue adding stock, in 1-cup batches, stirring until stock is absorbed after each addition. Total cooking time should be 20 minutes or until rice is tender. Stir in parmesan and extra butter. Season to taste.
6 Stir pine nuts into risotto with two-thirds of the rocket and half the cauliflower. Serve risotto topped with remaining rocket and cauliflower.

prep + cook time 35 minutes **serves** 4
nutritional count per serving 24.6g total fat (7.6g saturated fat); 23.96kJ (572 cal); 66.7g carbohydrate; 15.7g protein; 6.4g fibre

smoky chickpea stew

- 175g (5½ ounces) mini capsicums (bell peppers)
- ¼ cup (60ml) extra virgin olive oil
- 1 medium red onion (170g), chopped finely
- 2 cloves garlic, chopped finely
- pinch saffron threads
- 3 teaspoons paprika
- 1 cinnamon stick
- 800g (1½ pounds) canned chickpeas (garbanzo beans), drained, rinsed
- 400g (12½ ounces) canned diced tomatoes
- 2 cups (500ml) vegetable stock
- 200g (6½ ounces) green beans, halved lengthways
- 100g (3 ounces) baby rocket (arugula)

1 Preheat oven to 220°C/425°F.

2 Cut capsicums in half lengthways; remove seeds and membranes. Place capsicums on an oven tray; drizzle with 2 teaspoons of the oil. Roast 15 minutes or until tender.

3 Meanwhile, heat another 1 tablespoon of the oil in a deep large frying pan over medium heat; cook onion and garlic, stirring, 5 minutes or until soft. Add spices; cook, stirring, 1 minute or until fragrant.

4 Add chickpeas, tomatoes and stock to pan; bring to the boil. Reduce heat; simmer, uncovered, over low heat 12 minutes or until sauce thickens.

5 Add beans to chickpea mixture; simmer, uncovered, 2 minutes or until just tender. Season to taste. Serve stew topped with capsicum and rocket, drizzled with remaining oil.

prep + cook time 25 minutes **serves** 4
nutritional count per serving 17.6g total fat (2.7g saturated fat); 1460kJ (349 cal); 29.2g carbohydrate; 13.2g protein; 11.5g fibre
serving suggestion Grilled flatbread or couscous and Greek-style yoghurt.

za'atar spiced chickpea salad with fetta and mint

400g (12½ ounces) butternut pumpkin

1 large red onion (300g), cut into thin wedges

1 medium red capsicum (bell pepper) (200g), sliced thickly

1 medium yellow capsicum (bell pepper) (200g), sliced thickly

400g (12½ ounces) baby carrots, trimmed

2 tablespoons olive oil

400g (12½ ounces) canned chickpeas (garbanzo beans), drained, rinsed

2 tablespoons za'atar

¼ cup (60ml) red wine vinegar

¼ cup (60ml) olive oil, extra

100g (3 ounces) fetta, crumbled

⅓ cup lightly packed small fresh mint leaves

1 Preheat oven to 220°C/425°F.
2 Cut unpeeled pumpkin into thin wedges; halve crossways. Place pumpkin, onion, capsicum and carrot, in a single layer, on a baking-paper-lined large oven tray; drizzle with half the oil, then season. Bake 25 minutes or until tender.
3 Meanwhile, place chickpeas on another baking-paper-lined oven tray. Drizzle with remaining oil, sprinkle with za'atar; toss gently to coat. Bake 25 minutes or until golden and crisp.
4 Whisk vinegar and extra oil together in a small bowl; season to taste.
5 Place vegetables and chickpeas on a serving platter; drizzle with vinegar mixture, top with fetta and mint.

prep + cook time 40 minutes **serves** 4
nutritional count per serving 31g total fat (7.6g saturated fat); 1967kJ (470 cal); 28.9g carbohydrate; 13.1g protein; 13.6g fibre
tip It is important to have the vegetables in a single layer so they roast quickly without steaming. If necessary, divide the vegetables between two trays.
serving suggestion Grilled flatbread.

flatbreads with spinach, lentil and zucchini salad

- 1¼ cups (185g) plain (all-purpose) flour
- ½ cup (75g) self-raising flour
- pinch bicarbonate of soda (baking soda)
- 2 teaspoons caster (superfine) sugar
- 1 teaspoon black sesame seeds
- 1 teaspoon sea salt flakes
- ½ cup (140g) sour cream
- ⅓ cup (80ml) water
- 2 tablespoons vegetable oil
- 4 medium zucchini (480g), sliced thinly
- 400g (12½ ounces) canned lentils, drained, rinsed
- 50g (1½ ounces) baby spinach leaves
- ⅓ cup (110g) mango chilli chutney
- ¼ cup (40g) roasted unsalted cashews

cashew yoghurt

- ⅓ cup (50g) roasted unsalted cashews, chopped coarsely
- ¾ cup (200g) Greek-style yoghurt
- 2 tablespoons shredded fresh mint leaves
- 1 tablespoon lime juice

1 Sift flours and soda into a large bowl; stir in sugar, seeds and salt. Whisk sour cream, the water and half the oil together in a medium jug. Pour sour cream mixture into flour mixture; stir to combine. Knead dough until smooth; cover.

2 Cook zucchini on a heated oiled grill plate (or grill or barbecue) until tender. Transfer to a large bowl; add lentils and spinach, toss gently to combine. Season to taste.

3 Make cashew yoghurt.

4 Divide dough into four pieces; roll out on a floured surface into oval shapes about 2mm (⅛ inch) thick and 27.5cm (11 inches) long. Brush with remaining oil.

5 Cook dough on the heated oiled grill plate 2 minutes each side or until flatbreads are golden and cooked through.

6 Spread one side of flatbreads with chutney; top with lentil salad and cashew yoghurt. Sprinkle with cashews.

cashew yoghurt Combine ingredients in a small bowl; season to taste.

prep + cook time 40 minutes **serves** 4

nutritional count per serving 39.8g total fat (14g saturated fat); 3357kJ (802 cal); 86.2g carbohydrate; 20.4g protein; 8g fibre

kidney beans with eggs and coriander

italian bean stew

kidney beans with eggs and coriander

1 tablespoon olive oil

1 large red onion (300g), chopped finely

2 cloves garlic, chopped finely

1 large red capsicum (bell pepper) (350g), chopped finely

3 teaspoons mexican chilli powder

1 teaspoon smoked paprika

800g (1½ pounds) canned red kidney beans, drained, rinsed

400g (12½ ounces) canned diced tomatoes

½ cup (125ml) water

2 tablespoons brown sugar

1 tablespoon worcestershire sauce

4 eggs, hard-boiled

½ cup lightly packed fresh coriander (cilantro) sprigs

1 Heat oil in a deep large frying pan over medium heat; cook onion, garlic and capsicum, stirring, 5 minutes or until onion softens. Add chilli powder and paprika; cook, stirring, 1 minute or until fragrant.

2 Add beans, tomatoes, the water, sugar and sauce; bring to the boil. Reduce heat; simmer, uncovered, over low heat 10 minutes or until sauce thickens. Season to taste.

3 Meanwhile, place eggs in a small saucepan; cover with cold water. Bring to the boil; simmer, uncovered, 3 minutes. Drain; run under cold water until cool enough to handle. Peel eggs.

4 Tear eggs into pieces. Serve bean mixture topped with egg and coriander.

prep + cook time 25 minutes **serves** 4
nutritional count per serving 11.6g total fat (2.8g saturated fat); 1481kJ (354 cal); 36.5g carbohydrate; 20.3g protein; 14.3g fibre
serving suggestion Crusty bread, corn bread or tortillas.

italian bean stew

2½ tablespoons olive oil

1 medium red onion (170g), chopped finely

1 stick celery (150g), trimmed, chopped finely

1 medium carrot (120g), chopped finely

1 medium yellow capsicum (bell pepper) (200g), chopped

2 sprigs fresh rosemary

2 sprigs fresh thyme

10g (½ ounce) dried porcini mushrooms

½ cup (125ml) boiling water

800g (1½ pounds) canned borlotti beans, drained, rinsed

1½ cups (375ml) vegetable stock

250g (8 ounces) cherry tomatoes, halved

1 medium zucchini (120g), chopped coarsely

1 clove garlic, halved lengthways

8 slices ciabatta bread (400g)

⅓ cup (25g) finely grated parmesan

2 teaspoons fresh thyme leaves

1 Heat 1 tablespoon of the oil in a large saucepan over medium heat; cook onion, celery, carrot, capsicum and herbs 7 minutes or until vegetables soften.

2 Meanwhile, place mushrooms in a small heatproof bowl; cover with the boiling water. Stand 5 minutes or until softened.

3 Add beans, stock, tomatoes, zucchini, mushrooms and soaking liquid to pan; bring to the boil. Reduce heat; simmer, uncovered, over low heat 15 minutes or until thickened.

4 Meanwhile, preheat grill (broiler).

5 Rub cut-side of garlic over bread slices. Place on an oven tray, drizzle with remaining oil; scatter with parmesan. Grill 2 minutes or until golden.

6 Divide stew between bowls; serve with bread, and thyme.

prep + cook time 40 minutes **serves** 4
nutritional count per serving 16.7g total fat (3.4g saturated fat); 2175kJ (520 cal); 64.7g carbohydrate; 22g protein; 11.3g fibre

spicy red beans and rice

- 1½ cups (300g) basmati rice
- 1¾ cups (430ml) water
- 1 tablespoon olive oil
- 1 medium brown onion (150g), chopped finely
- 3 cloves garlic, chopped finely
- 1 stick celery (150g), trimmed, chopped coarsely
- 1 medium red capsicum (bell pepper) (200g), chopped coarsely
- 200g (6½ ounces) button mushrooms, quartered
- 200g (6½ ounces) swiss brown mushrooms
- 1 tablespoon mexican chilli powder
- 400g (12½ ounces) canned kidney beans, drained, rinsed
- 1 cup (250ml) water, extra
- 1 cup (250ml) tomato puree
- ½ cup (140g) sour cream
- 3 green onions (scallions), sliced thinly
- ½ cup lightly packed fresh coriander (cilantro) sprigs

1 Rinse rice in a sieve under cold water until water runs clear; drain well. Place rice in a medium saucepan with the water; season. Cover; bring to the boil. Reduce heat to low; cook, covered, 8 minutes or until tender.
2 Meanwhile, heat oil in a large saucepan over medium heat; cook onion, garlic, celery, capsicum and mushrooms, stirring, 5 minutes or until softened. Add chilli powder; cook, stirring, 1 minute or until fragrant.
3 Add beans, the extra water and puree to pan; bring to the boil. Reduce heat to low; simmer, uncovered, 15 minutes or until sauce thickens. Season to taste.
4 Divide rice and bean mixture between serving bowls. Serve topped with sour cream, green onion and coriander.

prep + cook time 40 minutes **serves** 4
nutritional count per serving 20.1g total fat (9.6g saturated fat); 2462kJ (588 cal); 80.3g carbohydrate; 16.5g protein; 10.8g fibre

pasta & couscous

Simple to make and full of fresh flavours, these hearty pasta and couscous recipes are filling meat-free dishes for everyone.

linguine primavera and poached eggs

- 180g (5½ ounces) podded broad (fava) beans
- 100g (3 ounces) snow peas, trimmed
- 2 teaspoons coarse cooking salt (kosher salt)
- 500g (1 pound) linguine
- ¼ cup (60ml) extra virgin olive oil
- 2 cloves garlic, sliced thinly
- 170g (5½ ounces) asparagus, cut into 5cm (2-inch) lengths
- 1 tablespoon white vinegar
- 4 eggs
- ¼ cup loosely packed fresh chervil leaves
- 1 cup (80g) finely grated parmesan

1 Drop broad beans into a large saucepan of boiling water; boil 2 minutes or until just tender. Remove beans with a slotted spoon. Rinse under cold water; drain well. Drop snow peas into the same water; boil 30 seconds or until bright green. Remove snow peas with a slotted spoon. Rinse under cold water; drain well. Remove shells from broad beans.

2 Return water to the boil, add salt. Cook pasta in boiling water 8 minutes or until just tender; drain. Return to pan to keep warm.

3 Meanwhile, heat 1 tablespoon of the oil in a large frying pan over medium high heat; cook garlic and asparagus, stirring, 2 minutes or until softened. Stir in broad beans and snow peas. Remove from heat.

4 Bring water to the boil in a deep frying pan; add vinegar. Break 1 egg into a cup, then slide into pan. When all eggs are in pan; return to the boil. Cover pan; remove from heat. Stand 3 minutes or until a light film of egg white sets over the eggs. Remove eggs from pan with a slotted spoon; drain on absorbent paper.

5 Return vegetable mixture to heat, add remaining oil and pasta; toss until heated through. Season to taste.

6 Serve linguine topped with poached egg, chervil, parmesan and freshly ground black pepper.

prep + cook time 30 minutes **serves** 4

nutritional count per serving 27.2g total fat (8.1g saturated fat); 3192kJ (763 cal); 91g carbohydrate, 33.3g protein; 8.7g fibre

tips We used fresh free-range eggs as they have thick egg whites that keep their shape while cooking.

You will need to buy about 750g (1½ pounds) broad beans in the pod for this recipe. Or, you can use 1½ cups (225g) frozen broad beans if you like.

spaghetti with mushrooms and breadcrumbs

¼ cup (60ml) extra virgin olive oil

140g (4½ ounces) sourdough bread, torn into small pieces

500g (1 pound) spaghetti

2 cloves garlic, sliced thinly

1 fresh long red chilli, sliced thinly

250g (8 ounces) mixed mushrooms, sliced thinly

1 tablespoon coarsely chopped fresh rosemary leaves

1 tablespoon coarsely chopped fresh thyme leaves

¼ cup loosely packed fresh sage leaves

1 cup (80g) shaved parmesan

1 Heat half the oil in a large frying pan over high heat; cook bread, stirring, 4 minutes or until golden brown. Drain on absorbent paper.

2 Cook spaghetti in a large saucepan of boiling salted water 8 minutes or until just tender. Reserve ¼ cup pasta water; drain. Return pasta to pan to keep warm.

3 Meanwhile, heat remaining oil in same frying pan; cook garlic, chilli and mushrooms 5 minutes or until mushrooms are tender. Stir in herbs; cook 1 minute.

4 Add reserved pasta water to spaghetti, then add mushroom mixture and bread; toss gently to combine. Season to taste. Serve pasta topped with parmesan.

prep + cook time 30 minutes **serves** 4

nutritional count per serving 22.9g total fat (6.4g saturated fat); 3167kJ (757 cal); 106.1g carbohydrate; 26.8g protein; 7.6g fibre

tip We used a combination of oyster, swiss brown, shiitake and button mushrooms.

zesty rocket and lemon pesto spaghetti

2 medium lemons (280g)

500g (1 pound) spaghetti

½ cup (75g) roasted unsalted cashews

⅓ cup (50g) roasted pine nuts

1 cup firmly packed fresh basil leaves

50g (1½ ounces) rocket (arugula)

1 teaspoon sea salt flakes

1¼ cups (100g) finely grated parmesan

1¼ cups (300ml) extra virgin olive oil

100g (3 ounces) rocket (arugula), extra

1 Finely grate rind from one lemon. Remove rind from remaining lemon with a zester (or cut rind into thin strips avoiding the white pith). Squeeze juice from lemons; you will need ¼ cup.

2 Cook spaghetti in a large saucepan of boiling salted water 8 minutes or until just tender; drain. Return to pan to keep warm.

3 Meanwhile, to make pesto, blend or process nuts, basil, rocket, juice, salt, 1 cup of the parmesan and 1 cup of the oil until almost smooth. Season to taste.

4 Heat remaining oil in a large frying pan. Add pesto, pasta and grated rind; toss until heated through.

5 Serve spaghetti sprinkled with extra rocket, remaining parmesan, lemon zest and, if you like, extra basil leaves.

prep + cook time 25 minutes **serves** 4

nutritional count per serving 96.4g total fat (18.1g saturated fat); 5698kJ (1360 cal); 92.9g carbohydrate; 28.8g protein; 7.5g fibre

tips You can use spaghettini or linguine for this recipe. The lemon in the pesto will discolour it quickly so use it immediately. If you wish to make it ahead, keep it covered tightly, then stir in the lemon just before serving.

spaghetti with mushrooms and breadcrumbs

zesty rocket and lemon pesto spaghetti

couscous, red cabbage and walnut salad

3 cups (600g) couscous
3 cups (750ml) boiling water
⅓ cup (35g) walnuts, chopped coarsely
2 tablespoons olive oil
200g (6½ ounces) red cabbage, shredded thinly
⅓ cup (55g) sultanas
100g (3 ounces) fetta, crumbled
100g (3 ounces) baby rocket (arugula) leaves

dressing

¼ cup (60ml) olive oil
2 tablespoons lemon juice
1 tablespoon dijon mustard

1 Combine couscous with the water in a large heatproof bowl; cover, stand 5 minutes. Fluff with a fork.

2 Meanwhile, make dressing.

3 Heat a large frying pan over high heat; cook nuts, stirring, 3 minutes or until roasted. Add oil, cabbage and sultanas; cook, stirring, a further 3 minutes or until cabbage begins to wilt.

4 Place cabbage mixture and couscous in a large heatproof bowl with fetta, rocket and dressing; toss gently to combine. Season to taste.

dressing Place ingredients in a screw-top jar; shake well. Season to taste.

prep + cook time 25 minutes **serves** 4

nutritional count per serving 35.9g total fat (8g saturated fat); 3916kJ (935 cal); 121.6g carbohydrate; 25.5g protein; 11g fibre

farfalle with creamy spiced roast capsicum sauce

- 2 teaspoons coriander seeds
- ½ teaspoon yellow mustard seeds
- 1 tablespoon olive oil
- 1 medium onion (150g), chopped finely
- 1 clove garlic, chopped finely
- 340g (11 ounces) bottled roasted capsicums (bell peppers), drained, sliced thinly
- 1 tablespoon tomato paste
- 400g (12½ ounces) canned crushed tomatoes
- 1 cup (250ml) water
- 500g (1 pound) farfalle pasta
- ½ cup (125ml) pouring cream
- 150g (4½ ounces) baby spinach leaves

1 Dry-fry seeds in a large saucepan over medium heat for 3 minutes or until fragrant. Transfer to a small heatproof bowl.

2 Heat oil in the same cleaned pan over medium heat; cook onion and garlic, stirring, 2 minutes or until onion softens. Add capsicum; cook 1 minute. Add paste, tomatoes and the water; bring to the boil. Reduce heat; simmer, uncovered, 25 minutes or until thickened. Season to taste.

3 Meanwhile, cook pasta in a large saucepan of boiling salted water 8 minutes or until just tender; drain. Return to the pan to keep warm.

4 Remove sauce from heat; stir in cream and seeds. Using a hand-held blender, blend sauce until smooth (reheat sauce if necessary). Add sauce to pasta with spinach; toss to combine. Season to taste. Serve topped with shaved parmesan, if you like.

prep + cook time 40 minutes **serves** 4

nutritional count per serving 18.6g total fat (8.4g saturated fat); 2724kJ (650 cal); 96.8g carbohydrate; 18.6g protein; 8.5g fibre

moroccan carrots with chickpeas and spinach couscous

- 10 baby carrots (200g)
- 1 tablespoon olive oil
- 2 teaspoons ground cumin
- 1 teaspoon ground paprika
- 1 teaspoon caster (superfine) sugar
- ½ cup (125ml) water
- 1¼ cups (250g) couscous
- 1¼ cups (310ml) boiling water
- 30g (1 ounce) butter, chopped
- 400g (12½ ounces) canned chickpeas (garbanzo beans), drained, rinsed
- 1 tablespoon lemon juice
- 50g (1½ ounces) baby spinach leaves, shredded
- 1 cup loosely packed fresh coriander (cilantro) leaves

1 Trim and peel carrots, leaving 3cm (1¼ inches) of the stem.
2 Heat oil in a medium saucepan over a medium heat; cook spices 30 seconds or until fragrant. Add carrots, sugar and the water; season to taste. Bring to the boil; simmer, partially covered, 12 minutes or until carrots are tender.
3 Meanwhile, combine couscous with the boiling water in a large heatproof bowl; cover; stand 3 minutes. Fluff with a fork. Cover, stand a further 3 minutes; fluff with a fork. Stir in butter; season to taste.
4 Add chickpeas to pan with carrots; cook, covered, 3 minutes or until heated through. Stir in juice.
5 Stir spinach through couscous; spoon onto a shallow serving dish. Top with carrot mixture and coriander.

prep + cook time 30 minutes **serves** 4
nutritional count per serving 12.8g total fat (4.9g saturated fat); 1770kJ (423 cal); 59.7g carbohydrate; 12.8g protein; 8.6g fibre
serving suggestion Greek-style yoghurt and harissa.

sesame and peanut soba noodles

2 tablespoons sesame seeds

450g (14½ ounces) soba noodles

¼ cup (60ml) peanut oil

100g (3 ounces) choy sum

1 clove garlic, crushed

2 fresh long red chillies, sliced thinly

4 green onions (scallions), sliced thinly

¼ cup (70g) crunchy peanut butter

¼ cup (60ml) soy sauce

¼ cup (60ml) oyster-flavoured sauce

2 tablespoons chinese cooking wine (shao hsing)

100g (3 ounces) sugar snap peas, trimmed

1 green onion (scallion), sliced thinly, extra

1 Toast sesame seeds in a heated wok over medium heat, stirring, until golden. Remove from wok.
2 Cook noodles in a large saucepan of boiling salted water 2 minutes or until just tender. Reserve 1 cup cooking liquid; drain. Combine noodles with 1 tablespoon of the oil in a medium bowl; cover to keep warm.
3 Meanwhile, trim choy sum; cut into 10cm (4-inch) lengths.
4 Heat remaining oil in a large wok; stir-fry garlic, half the chilli and onion until fragrant. Add peanut butter, sauces, wine and reserved cooking liquid; bring to the boil. Add snap peas; cook, stirring, 1 minute. Add choy sum and noodles; toss until choy sum is wilted. Serve sprinkled with remaining chilli, toasted seeds and extra onion.

prep + cook time 25 minutes **serves** 4
nutritional count per serving 27g total fat (4.5g saturated fat); 1915kJ (457 cal); 33.7g carbohydrate; 14.6g protein; 10.9g fibre
tip Choose an oyster-flavoured sauce without any seafood content. Check the label if you are unsure.

bean and leek risoni

375g (12 ounces) risoni pasta

2 tablespoons olive oil

1 medium leek (350g), sliced

1 clove garlic, crushed

½ cup (125ml) dry white wine

400g (12½ ounces) canned borlotti beans, drained, rinsed

400g (12½ ounces) canned butter beans, drained, rinsed

1 cup (250ml) vegetable stock

150g (4½ ounces) fresh green beans, cut into 5cm (2-inch) lengths

150g (4½ ounces) fresh butter beans, cut into 5cm (2-inch) lengths

1 tablespoon finely grated lemon rind

¼ cup (60ml) lemon juice

½ cup torn fresh flat-leaf parsley

⅓ cup (25g) finely grated parmesan

1 Cook risoni in a large saucepan of boiling salted water until tender; drain.
2 Meanwhile, heat oil in a deep large saucepan over medium heat; cook leek and garlic, stirring, 5 minutes or until leek is softened. Increase heat to high, add wine; cook, stirring, until liquid is almost evaporated.
3 Add canned beans and stock; bring to the boil. Add fresh beans, reduce heat; simmer, stirring occasionally, 3 minutes or until just tender. Stir in risoni until heated through. Stir in rind, juice, parsley and parmesan. Season to taste. Sprinkle with a little extra parmesan, if you like.

prep + cook time 30 minutes **serves** 4
nutritional count per serving 13.7g total fat (3.1g saturated fat); 2448kJ (585 cal); 82.4g carbohydrate; 22.6g protein; 14.1g fibre

sesame and peanut soba noodles

bean and leek risoni

linguine with squash, baby brussels sprouts and spring onions

150g (4½ ounces) baby brussels sprouts

500g (1 pound) linguine

2 tablespoons extra virgin olive oil

400g (12½ ounces) baby spring onions, trimmed, halved

1 clove garlic, sliced

100g (3 ounces) yellow patty-pan squash, sliced thinly

1 cup (120g) frozen peas

2 tablespoons finely grated lemon rind

100g (3 ounces) goat's cheese, crumbled

1 Separate as many of the outer leaves from brussels sprouts as possible; cut hearts of sprouts in half.

2 Cook pasta in a large saucepan of boiling salted water 8 minutes or until just tender; drain. Return to pan to keep warm.

3 Meanwhile, heat oil in a large frying pan over medium heat; cook onions and garlic, stirring, 5 minutes or until onions are tender and golden. Add sprout hearts, squash and peas; cook, stirring, 2 minutes. Add rind, sprout leaves and pasta to pan; cook, tossing, until pasta is heated through and sprout leaves are just tender. Season to taste.

4 Divide mixture between serving bowls; top with cheese.

prep + cook time 25 minutes **serves** 4

nutritional count per serving 17g total fat (5.4g saturated fat); 2759kJ (660 cal); 95.9g carbohydrate; 24.4g protein; 11.1g fibre

wholemeal spaghetti with green lentils, mushrooms and parsley butter

- 1 cup (200g) French-style green lentils
- 500g (1 pound) wholemeal spaghetti
- 2 teaspoons coarse salt
- 2 tablespoons extra virgin olive oil
- 2 shallots (50g), sliced thinly
- 1 clove garlic, crushed
- 250g (8 ounces) oyster mushrooms, sliced thickly
- 30g (1 ounce) butter
- ¾ cup loosely packed fresh flat-leaf parsley leaves

1 Cook lentils in a large saucepan of boiling water 20 minutes. Add spaghetti and salt; cook until spaghetti is just tender. Drain; return to pan to keep warm.

2 Meanwhile, heat oil in a large frying pan over medium heat; cook shallots and garlic, stirring, 1 minute or until fragrant. Add mushrooms; cook, stirring occasionally, further 5 minutes or until mushrooms are tender and browned lightly.

3 Add butter to mushroom mixture; stir over high heat until butter is melted. Stir in pasta mixture and half the parsley; toss until heated through. Season to taste.

4 Serve spaghetti sprinkled with remaining parsley.

prep + cook time 40 minutes **serves** 4

nutritional count per serving 18.3g total fat (5.9g saturated fat); 3097kJ (740 cal); 107.9g carbohydrate; 30.5g protein; 11.5g fibre

fettuccine with burnt sage butter, roasted artichokes and garlic

20 marinated artichoke hearts (560g), halved

4 cloves garlic, sliced

¼ cup (60ml) olive oil

500g (1 pound) fettuccine

30g (1 ounce) butter

⅓ cup loosely packed fresh sage leaves

⅔ cup (50g) thinly shaved pecorino cheese

1 Preheat oven to 220°C/425°F.

2 Place artichokes on a baking-paper-lined oven tray; sprinkle with garlic and oil. Roast 10 minutes or until browned.

3 Meanwhile, cook pasta in a large saucepan of boiling salted water 8 minutes or until just tender; drain. Return to pan to keep warm.

4 Melt butter in a large frying pan over medium-high heat; cook sage leaves 1 minute or until butter begins to change colour. Remove sage from the pan. Add pasta and artichokes to pan; toss to combine. Season to taste.

5 Sprinkle pasta with sage; serve with cheese.

prep + cook time 45 minutes **serves** 4

nutritional count per serving 25.7g total fat (7.4g saturated fat); 3020kJ (721 cal); 90.2g carbohydrate; 22.5g protein; 18.1g fibre

tip You can use drained canned artichokes, if you like.

couscous with spiced eggplant and lemony yoghurt

4 medium eggplants (1.2kg), halved, sliced thinly
4 cloves garlic, crushed
1 tablespoon za'atar
3 teaspoons ground cumin
2 teaspoons ground coriander
2 teaspoons ground turmeric
¾ teaspoon chilli flakes
½ cup (125ml) olive oil
⅓ cup (80ml) cold water
1½ cups (300g) couscous
1 tablespoon extra virgin olive oil
1½ cups (375ml) boiling water
½ cup loosely packed fresh coriander (cilantro) sprigs

lemony yoghurt
1 cup (280g) natural yoghurt
1 tablespoon finely grated lemon rind
1 tablespoon lemon juice
1 clove garlic, crushed

1 Preheat oven to 200°C/400°F.
2 Place eggplant, garlic, spices and chilli in a large roasting pan; drizzle with combined olive oil and the cold water. Roast 25 minutes, stirring halfway through, or until eggplant is golden and tender. Season to taste.
3 Meanwhile, place couscous in a heatproof bowl, drizzle with extra virgin olive oil; using your fingertips, rub oil into couscous. Stir in the boiling water; cover, stand 10 minutes. Fluff with a fork; season to taste.
4 Make lemony yoghurt.
5 Serve couscous topped with eggplant mixture, lemony yoghurt, coriander and a little extra za'atar.
lemony yoghurt Combine ingredients in a small bowl.

prep + cook time 35 minutes **serves** 4
nutritional count per serving 38.4g total fat (7.3g saturated fat); 2930kJ (700 cal); 65.9g carbohydrate; 16.3g protein; 12g fibre

spaghetti with radicchio, pear, blue cheese and walnuts

- 500g (1 pound) spaghetti
- ½ cup (50g) walnuts
- 50g (1½ ounces) butter
- 2 baby pears (200g), halved, cored, sliced thinly
- 1 clove garlic, crushed
- ⅔ cup (160ml) pouring cream
- 1 medium radicchio (200g), leaves separated, torn
- 80g (2½ ounces) blue cheese, crumbled

1 Cook pasta in a large saucepan of boiling salted water 8 minutes or until just tender; drain. Return to pan to keep warm.

2 Meanwhile, toast walnuts in a large frying pan over medium heat 5 minutes or until browned lightly. Chop coarsely.

3 Melt butter in same frying pan over medium-high heat; cook pear, stirring, 2 minutes or until beginning to caramelise. Add garlic; cook, stirring, until fragrant. Stir in cream; bring to the boil.

4 Add pasta, radicchio and half the nuts to pear mixture, sprinkle with cheese; toss gently to combine. Season to taste. Serve pasta sprinkled with remaining nuts.

prep + cook time 30 minutes **serves** 4
nutritional count per serving 42g total fat (18.7g saturated fat); 3592kJ (858 cal); 95.2g carbohydrate; 21.5g protein; 7.2g fibre
tip We used corella pears.

watercress and goat's cheese ravioli

- **3 medium lemons (420g)**
- **⅓ cup (35g) walnuts**
- **1 cup (120g) firmly packed trimmed watercress**
- **80g (2½ ounces) butter**
- **240g (7½ ounces) goat's cheese**
- **1 egg, beaten lightly**
- **275g (9 ounces) round gow gee wrappers**
- **50g (1½ ounces) bull's blood leaves**

1 Finely grate rind from two lemons, you need 1½ tablespoons. Remove rind from remaining lemon with a zester (or cut rind into thin strips avoiding the white pith). Squeeze juice from lemons; you will need ¼ cup.

2 Meanwhile, roast nuts in a large frying pan over medium heat about 5 minutes or until browned lightly. Chop coarsely.

3 Coarsely chop ¾ cup of the watercress. Heat 20g (¾ ounce) of the butter in a large frying pan over high heat; cook watercress, stirring, about 30 seconds or until beginning to wilt.

4 Place cooked watercress in a medium bowl with cheese, egg, 1 tablespoon of the rind and 1 tablespoon of the juice; toss to combine. Season to taste.

5 Working with a few wrappers at a time, brush edges with water using a pastry brush. Place a heaped teaspoon of the cheese mixture in the centre of each wrapper. Fold wrappers in half to enclose pastry, pinching edges to seal.

6 Drop ravioli into a large saucepan of boiling salted water in batches; simmer, uncovered, about 2 minutes or until wrappers are just transparent. Remove ravioli with a large slotted spoon; drain. Divide between warmed serving bowls.

7 Melt remaining butter in a large frying pan over high heat until beginning to brown. Immediately stir in remaining rind and remaining juice. Season to taste. Spoon sauce over ravioli.

8 Serve ravioli topped with remaining watercress, bull's blood leaves, lemon zest and nuts .

prep + cook time 45 minutes **serves** 4
nutritional count per serving 37g total fat (19.9g saturated fat); 2473kJ (590 cal); 41.9g carbohydrate; 22g protein; 2.3g fibre

14 0 1 2
13 3
12 4
11 5
7 6
TEASPOON

curries

One of the best things about vegetarian cooking is its ability to take on flavours from around the world, such as Asia.

yellow dhal with spinach

- 60g (2 ounces) ghee (clarified butter)
- 1 teaspoon cumin seeds
- 1 teaspoon ground turmeric
- ¾ teaspoon ground chilli
- 2 shallots (50g), sliced thinly
- 2 cloves garlic, crushed
- 4cm (1½-inch) piece fresh ginger (20g), grated
- 2 long green chillies, sliced thinly
- 200g (6½ ounces) yellow lentils (channa dhal)
- 1.25 litres (5 cups) water
- 60g (2 ounces) baby spinach leaves

1 Heat ghee in a large saucepan over medium heat; cook spices, stirring, 1 minute or until fragrant.

2 Add shallots, garlic, ginger and half the chilli; cook, stirring, about 3 minutes or until softened.

3 Meanwhile, wash lentils under running water until water runs clear; drain well. Add lentils to pan; stir until combined. Add the water; cover, bring to the boil. Reduce heat to medium low, or a brisk simmer; cook, covered, 30 minutes or until lentils are soft and have broken down, stirring occasionally.

4 Add spinach; stir until wilted. Season to taste. Serve topped with remaining chilli.

prep + cook time 40 minutes **serves** 4

nutritional count per serving 16.5g total fat (10g saturated fat); 1237kJ (296 cal); 20.9g carbohydrate; 13.3g protein; 8.5g fibre

tip Add more water if the dhal is too thick. You could replace 3 cups of the water with vegetable stock, if you like.

serving suggestion Serve with roti

cauliflower and chickpea curry

1 small cauliflower (1kg), cut into small florets

2 tablespoons vegetable oil

4cm (1½-inch) piece fresh ginger (20g), grated finely

2 cloves garlic, crushed

1 teaspoon garam masala

½ teaspoon ground turmeric

2 medium tomatoes (300g), chopped finely

200g (6½ ounces) Greek-style yoghurt

400g (12½ ounces) canned chickpeas (garbanzo beans), drained, rinsed

¼ cup loosely packed fresh coriander (cilantro) sprigs

1 Cook cauliflower in a medium saucepan of boiling salted water; simmer 4 minutes or until almost tender. Drain well.
2 Meanwhile, heat oil in a medium saucepan over medium heat; cook ginger, garlic and spices 1 minute or until fragrant. Add tomato; simmer, uncovered, 5 minutes or until tomato has broken down. Stir in yoghurt, then cauliflower and chickpeas. Simmer, covered, 5 minutes or until cauliflower is tender. Season to taste.
3 Serve curry sprinkled with coriander.

prep + cook time 25 minutes **serves** 4
nutritional count per serving 14.2g total fat (3.2g saturated fat); 1206kJ (288 cal); 22.8g carbohydrate; 12g protein; 10.2g fibre
serving suggestion Naan bread, chapatti or roti, or steamed basmati rice.

thai eggplant curry

250g (8 ounces) thai eggplant, quartered

2 baby (finger) eggplants (120g), sliced

1 small eggplant (230g), cut into thick batons

1 tablespoon vegetable oil

4 shallots (100g), sliced thinly

10cm (4-inch) stick fresh lemon grass (20g), halved lengthways, bruised

¼ cup (75g) green curry paste

1 cup (250ml) coconut milk

½ cup (125ml) water

4 fresh kaffir lime leaves

30g (1 ounce) fresh thai basil leaves

1 fresh long red chilli, sliced thinly

1 Steam all eggplant 8 minutes or until almost tender.
2 Meanwhile, heat oil in a medium saucepan over medium heat; cook shallot and lemon grass 3 minutes until softened. Add curry paste; cook, stirring, 1 minute or until fragrant.
3 Stir in coconut milk, the water and lime leaves; bring to a simmer. Add eggplant; cook, covered, 5 minutes or until eggplant is tender.
4 Stir half the basil leaves into curry. Season to taste.
5 Serve curry sprinkled with chilli and remaining basil leaves.

prep + cook time 25 minutes **serves** 4
nutritional count per serving 18.2g total fat (10g saturated fat); 886kJ (212 cal); 6.6g carbohydrate; 3.5g protein; 4.6g fibre
tip Thai eggplant is also known as makeua prao; golf-ball sized eggplants available in different colours, but most commonly green traced in off-white. They are found in Asian grocery stores.
serving suggestion Steamed jasmine rice.

cauliflower and chickpea curry

thai eggplant curry

breakfast curry

- 2 large desiree potatoes (600g)
- 1 tablespoon vegetable oil
- 2 sprigs curry leaves
- 2 teaspoons brown mustard seeds
- 1 teaspoon ground turmeric
- ½ teaspoon ground cumin
- 1 medium brown onion (150g), sliced thinly
- 2cm (¾-inch) piece fresh ginger (10g), grated finely
- 3 medium tomatoes (450g), chopped coarsely
- 2 tablespoons desiccated coconut
- ¼ cup (60ml) water
- 4 eggs

1 Peel potatoes. Place potatoes in microwave-safe bowl; sprinkle with a little water. Microwave potatoes, covered, on HIGH (100%) 3 minutes. Cool slightly; cut into 1.5cm (¾-inch) cubes.

2 Meanwhile, heat oil in a medium saucepan over medium heat; cook curry leaves 1 minute or until crisp. Remove from pan with a slotted spoon. Add spices; cook, stirring, a further 30 seconds. Add onion to pan with ginger; cook, stirring, about 3 minutes or until softened.

3 Add tomato to pan with potato, coconut and the water; cook, covered, over low heat about 10 minutes or until potato is tender. Season to taste.

4 Meanwhile, bring water to the boil in a deep frying pan. Break one egg into a cup then slide into pan. When all eggs are in the pan; return to the boil. Cover pan; remove from heat. Stand 3 minutes or until a light film of egg white sets over the eggs. Remove from pan with a slotted spoon; drain on absorbent paper.

5 Divide potato mixture between serving bowls; top with eggs and curry leaves.

prep + cook time 25 minutes **serves** 4
nutritional count per serving 12.5g total fat (4g saturated fat); 1083kJ (259 cal); 20.9g carbohydrate; 12.6g protein; 4.8g fibre
tip We used fresh free range eggs as they have thick egg whites that keep their shape while cooking.
serving suggestion Top with fresh coriander (cilantro) leaves and serve with naan bread, chapatti or roti.

japanese pumpkin curry

¼ medium jap pumpkin (750g)
⅓ cup (50g) plain (all-purpose) flour
6 eggs
1½ cups (225g) panko (japanese) breadcrumbs
1 cup (200g) medium grain white rice
1¼ cups (310ml) water
1 teaspoon salt
2 tablespoons vegetable oil
1 medium brown onion (150g), sliced thinly
100g (3 ounces) medium-hot japanese curry mix
2½ cups (625ml) water, extra
1 cup (150g) shelled edamame
1 teaspoon black or toasted white sesame seeds

1 Cut pumpkin into four 2cm (¾-inch) thick wedges. Remove seeds and skin. Steam pumpkin 10 minutes or until tender, turning halfway. Pat pumpkin pieces dry with absorbent paper.
2 Toss pumpkin in flour; shake off excess. Lightly beat two of the eggs in a shallow bowl; dip pumpkin into egg, then coat in breadcrumbs. Place on a baking-paper-lined oven tray.
3 Place rice, the water and salt in a medium saucepan; bring to the boil over high heat. Cover with a tight-fitting lid; cook over low heat 8 minutes or until rice is tender. Remove from heat.
4 Meanwhile, heat half the oil in a medium saucepan over medium heat; cook onion, stirring, 3 minutes or until softened. Stir in curry mix and the extra water; cook 5 minutes. Stir in edamame; cook 2 minutes or until heated through.
5 Place remaining eggs in a small saucepan; add enough cold water to cover. Bring to the boil, stirring, to centre the yolks. Simmer, uncovered, 2 minutes for soft-boiled. Drain; rinse eggs under cold water until cool enough to handle. Peel eggs.
6 Heat remaining oil in a large frying pan over medium heat; cook pumpkin 2 minutes each side or until golden.
7 Fluff rice with a fork. Divide rice between serving bowls; spoon curry to the side. Top with pumpkin and torn eggs; sprinkle with seeds.

prep + cook time 40 minutes **serves** 4
nutritional count per serving 31.9g total fat (9.4g saturated fat); 3762kJ (899 cal); 117.2g carbohydrate; 32g protein; 6.1g fibre
tips Both Japanese curry mix and frozen edamame (soy beans in the pod) are available from Asian supermarkets.
You will need to shell about 300g (9½ ounces) frozen edamame in the pod for this recipe.

potato and egg rendang

red tofu curry

potato and egg rendang

- 1 medium brown onion (150g), chopped finely
- 185g (6 ounces) rendang curry paste
- 1 cup (250ml) coconut milk
- ½ cup (125ml) water
- 3 medium desiree potatoes (750g), chopped coarsely
- 1 tablespoon vegetable oil
- 4 eggs
- 1 cup lightly packed fresh coriander (cilantro) leaves

1 Cook onion and curry paste in a medium saucepan over medium heat, stirring, 3 minutes or until onion has softened and paste is fragrant.
2 Stir in coconut milk and the water; bring to a simmer. Add potato; cook, covered, 15 minutes or until tender, stirring occasionally. Season to taste.
3 Meanwhile, heat oil in a large frying pan over medium-high heat; break eggs into pan. Cook eggs until done as desired.
4 Divide curry between serving bowls; top with fried eggs and coriander.

prep + cook time 15 minutes **serves** 4
nutritional count per serving 26.6g total fat (12.4g saturated fat); 1724kJ (412 cal); 27.4g carbohydrate; 13.9g protein; 4g fibre
serving suggestion Steamed rice or roti.

red tofu curry

- 1 tablespoon vegetable oil
- 1 medium red onion (170g), sliced thinly
- ⅓ cup (100g) red curry paste
- 1 cup (250ml) coconut milk
- ½ cup (125ml) water
- 1 bunch baby carrots (400g), trimmed
- 175g (5½ ounces) broccolini, trimmed
- 200g (6½ ounces) fried tofu puffs, halved
- 100g (3 ounces) snow peas, trimmed
- 1 cup lightly packed fresh coriander (cilantro) sprigs

1 Heat oil in a medium saucepan over medium heat; cook onion, stirring, 3 minutes until softened slightly.
2 Add curry paste, coconut milk, the water and carrots to pan, bring to a simmer; cook, stirring, 4 minutes. Add broccolini and tofu puffs; cook 2 minutes. Add snow peas; simmer, 1 minute or until just tender. Season to taste.
3 Serve curry topped with coriander.

prep + cook time 15 minutes **serves** 4
nutritional count per serving 22.4g total fat (13g saturated fat); 1250kJ (298 cal); 13.1g carbohydrate; 11.6g protein; 11.5g fibre
serving suggestion Steamed jasmine rice.

vegie curry pies

- 1 tablespoon vegetable oil
- 1 medium brown onion (150g), sliced
- 2 tablespoons penang curry paste
- 1 cup (250ml) coconut milk
- 2 baby (finger) eggplants (120g), peeled, sliced
- 1 medium desiree potato (200g), cut into 1.5cm (¾-inch) cubes
- 1 small kumara (orange sweet potato) (250g), cut into 1.5cm (¾-inch) cubes
- 1 tablespoon lime juice
- 1 teaspoon sesame oil
- ½ cup (75g) coarsely chopped roasted cashews
- 1 cup (120g) frozen peas
- 2 sheets puff pastry
- 1 egg, beaten lightly

1 Preheat oven to 200°C/400°F.
2 Heat vegetable oil in a medium saucepan or wok over medium-high heat; cook onion, stirring, 3 minutes or until softened. Add curry paste; cook a further 2 minutes or until fragrant. Stir in coconut milk; bring to a simmer. Add eggplant, potato and kumara; cook, covered, 10 minutes or until vegetables are tender. Remove from heat; stir in juice, sesame oil, nuts and peas; season to taste. Spread mixture in a shallow tray; cool in freezer about 5 minutes.
3 Meanwhile, using one of four 1 cup (250ml) ramekins as a guide, cut four rounds from pastry, 2cm (¾ inch) larger than the dish.
4 Spoon curry mixture evenly into ramekins. Lightly brush outer rims of ramekins with a little egg; cover with pastry lids, pressing overhanging pastry against the sides. Brush pastry with a little more egg. Cut a small slit in the top of each pie. Place pies on an oven tray.
5 Bake pies 15 minutes or until golden.

prep + cook time 45 minutes **makes** 4
nutritional count per pie 50.1g total fat (24.7g saturated fat); 3222kJ (770 cal); 59.4g carbohydrate; 15.9g protein; 7.8g fibre
serving suggestion Tomato, onion and coriander sambal or a mixed leaf salad.

vegetable curry omelette rolls

- 1 tablespoon vegetable oil
- ¼ cup (75g) massaman curry paste
- 2 cups (500ml) coconut milk
- 2 teaspoons sesame oil
- 1 medium carrot (120g), grated coarsely
- 1 medium red capsicum (bell pepper) (200g), cut into matchsticks
- 230g (7 ounces) baby corn, halved lengthways
- 3 eggs
- 1 tablespoon water
- ½ cup (40g) bean sprouts
- ¼ cup lightly packed fresh mint leaves
- ¼ cup lightly packed fresh thai basil leaves

1 Heat half the vegetable oil in a medium saucepan over medium heat; cook paste 2 minutes or until fragrant. Stir in coconut milk and sesame oil; bring to a simmer. Add carrot, capsicum and corn; simmer, uncovered, 3 minutes or until tender. Season to taste.

2 Meanwhile, heat 1 teaspoon of the remaining vegetable oil in a small 20cm (8-inch) (base measurement) non-stick frying pan over medium heat. Whisk eggs with the water. Pour half the egg mixture into pan, swirl to coat base; cook 1 minute or until golden underneath. Turn or flip omelette, cook for a further 30 seconds. Transfer omelette to a warmed plate; repeat with remaining vegetable oil and egg mixture.

3 Divide vegetable mixture, half the curry mixture and sprouts between omelettes; fold omelette over. Spoon over remaining curry mixture; sprinkle with herbs.

prep + cook time 20 minutes **serves** 2
nutritional count per serving 79.8g total fat (42.8g saturated fat); 3730kJ (891 cal); 19.8g carbohydrate; 21.6g protein; 9.1g fibre
tip You can also cut the carrot into thin strips using an Asian julienne vegetable peeler, available from Asian food stores.

weekend specials

These recipes may take more kitchen-time, but that just makes them perfect for impressive weekend entertaining with friends.

caramelised onion and fennel soup with twice-baked cheese soufflés

60g (2 ounces) butter

1kg (2 pounds) brown onions, sliced thinly

1 medium fennel (300g), sliced thinly

1 teaspoon fresh thyme leaves

1 teaspoon brown sugar

1 litre (4 cups) vegetable stock

2 cups (500ml) water

twice-baked cheese soufflés

50g (1½ ounces) butter, chopped

⅓ cup (50g) plain (all-purpose) flour

1½ cups (375ml) milk

1 cup (120g) grated vintage cheddar

3 eggs, separated

⅓ cup (80ml) pouring cream

1 Heat butter in a large saucepan over medium heat; cook onion, fennel and thyme, covered, 20 minutes or until very soft. Add sugar; cook, stirring occasionally, 20 minutes or until onion and fennel are caramelised.

2 Meanwhile, make twice-baked cheese soufflés.

3 Stir stock and the water into onion mixture; bring to the boil. Reduce heat; simmer, covered, 5 minutes. Season to taste.

4 Place soufflés in serving bowls; pour soup around soufflés. Serve topped with some extra thyme.

twice-baked cheese soufflés Preheat oven to 180°C/350°F. Grease six ⅔ cup (160ml) metal dariole moulds or soufflé dishes; line bases with baking paper. Melt butter in a medium saucepan over medium heat, add flour; cook, stirring, 1 minute. Gradually stir in milk; stir until mixture boils and thickens. Transfer mixture to a medium heatproof bowl. Stir in ¾ cup of the cheddar, then egg yolks. Season to taste. Beat egg whites in a small bowl with an electric mixer until soft peaks form. Fold egg white into cheese mixture, in two batches. Spoon mixture into dishes. Place dishes in a small baking dish; add enough boiling water to the baking dish to come halfway up side of the dishes. Bake soufflés 15 minutes or until firm. Stand soufflés 5 minutes; turn soufflés out into a baking-paper-lined ovenproof dish. Cool. Spoon cream over soufflés; top with remaining cheddar. Bake further 15 minutes or until puffed and browned.

prep + cook time 1 hour (+ cooling) **serves** 6

nutritional count per serving 32.6g total fat (16.7g saturated fat); 1852kJ (442 cal); 20.4g carbohydrate; 16.4g protein; 4g fibre

tip Soufflés can be baked the first time 8 hours ahead. Bake for the second time just before serving. The soup can be made a day ahead.

mushroom and water chestnut steamed wontons

- 2 teaspoons sesame oil
- 200g (6½ ounces) button mushrooms, chopped finely
- 100g (3 ounces) woodear mushrooms, chopped finely
- 200g (6½ ounces) enoki mushrooms, trimmed, chopped finely
- 3 green onions (scallions), chopped finely
- 5cm (2-inch) piece fresh ginger (25g), grated
- 2 tablespoons light soy sauce
- 1 teaspoon finely grated lemon rind
- 2 tablespoons finely chopped canned water chestnuts
- 36 wonton wrappers

warm dipping sauce

- 1 tablespoon sesame oil
- 1 green onion (scallion), sliced
- 1 fresh long red chilli, sliced
- 5cm (2-inch) piece fresh ginger (25g), cut into thin matchsticks
- 1 cup (250ml) light soy sauce
- 1 teaspoon finely grated lemon rind

1 Heat oil in a large frying pan over medium heat; cook mushrooms, onion and ginger over high heat, stirring, until mushrooms are soft. Add sauce; cook until evaporated. Remove from heat; stir in rind and water chestnuts. Cool.
2 Working in batches, place wrappers on a board. Place 2 level teaspoons of mushroom mixture in the centre of each wrapper. Brush a little water around the edges of each wrapper; bring four corners in to the centre, then press edges together to seal.
3 Line a bamboo steamer with baking paper; place wontons in steamer. Place steamer over a wok or large saucepan of simmering water; cover, steam wontons 5 minutes or until heated through.
4 Meanwhile, make warm dipping sauce.
5 Serve wontons with dipping sauce.
warm dipping sauce Heat oil in a small frying pan over medium heat; cook onion, chilli and ginger for 30 seconds. Stir in sauce and rind. Remove from heat.

prep + cook time 45 minutes (+ cooling) **serves** 6
nutritional count per serving 5.7g total fat (0.8g saturated fat); 1270kJ (303 cal); 48.8g carbohydrate; 12.1g protein; 9.8g fibre
tips Woodear mushrooms are a type of Asian mushroom. They are available from Asian food stores and specialty greengrocers.
The wontons can be made several hours ahead; keep refrigerated in a single layer on a tray, without touching.

greek baked eggplant

- 2 large eggplants (1kg), halved lengthways
- 2 tablespoons olive oil
- ½ medium red onion (85g), chopped finely
- 1 stick celery (150g), trimmed, chopped finely
- 1 clove garlic, crushed
- 2 teaspoons finely chopped fresh oregano leaves
- 1 large red capsicum (bell pepper) (350g), chopped finely
- 2 medium roma (egg) tomatoes (150g), chopped finely
- 1 teaspoon finely grated lemon rind
- 1 teaspoon lemon juice
- 100g (3 ounces) fetta, crumbled
- ⅔ cup (100g) pitted black olives, chopped finely
- ¾ cup (55g) panko (japanese) breadcrumbs
- ¾ cup (60g) finely grated parmesan
- 1 tablespoon coarsely chopped fresh flat-leaf parsley

1 Preheat oven to 220°C/425°F. Line two oven trays with baking paper.

2 Using a small knife, cut a 1cm (½-inch) border inside each eggplant half; scoop out the flesh without breaking the skin. Reserve flesh for another use. Place eggplant shells, cut-side-up on oven trays; cover with foil. Bake 25 minutes.

3 Meanwhile, heat half the oil in a large frying pan over medium heat; cook onion, celery, garlic and oregano, stirring, 3 minutes or until soft. Add capsicum; cook, stirring, 3 minutes or until soft. Stir in tomato, rind and juice; remove from heat. Stir in fetta and olives; season to taste.

4 Combine breadcrumbs, parmesan and parsley in a small bowl; season to taste.

5 Reduce oven to 200°C/400°F.

6 Spoon capsicum mixture into eggplant halves; top with breadcrumb mixture. Bake 25 minutes or until eggplant is tender. Drizzle with remaining oil before serving.

prep + cook time 1 hour **serves** 4

nutritional count per serving 21.1g total fat (8g saturated fat); 1515kJ (362 cal); 21.2g carbohydrate; 16.6g protein; 9.8g fibre

serving suggestion A green leaf salad.

pumpkin and ricotta bake

500g (1 pound) jap pumpkin, chopped coarsely

1 small red onion (80g), sliced

1 fresh long red chilli, seeded, sliced

½ teaspoon ground cinnamon

2 tablespoons olive oil

1 cup (240g) fresh ricotta

⅓ cup (50g) pine nuts

400g (12½ ounces) fresh borlotti beans, shelled

½ cup (35g) panko (japanese) breadcrumbs

½ cup (40g) finely grated parmesan

1 teaspoon finely grated lemon rind

2 tablespoons olive oil, extra

175g (5½ ounces) broccolini, halved lengthways

½ cup loosely packed fresh flat-leaf parsley leaves, chopped coarsely

1 Preheat oven to 220°C/425°F.

2 Place pumpkin in four shallow 2-cup (500ml) ovenproof pans or dishes with onion, chilli and cinnamon; drizzle with oil. Season; toss to combine. Drop spoonfuls of ricotta onto pumpkin. Roast 25 minutes or until pumpkin is just tender.

3 Meanwhile, place pine nuts on an oven tray; roast 3 minutes or until browned lightly. Cool.

4 Place beans in a medium saucepan with enough water to cover; bring to the boil. Reduce heat; simmer, uncovered, over low heat, 20 minutes or until tender; drain.

5 Combine breadcrumbs, parmesan, rind and extra oil in a small bowl; season.

6 Sprinkle beans over pumpkin; arrange broccolini on top, then sprinkle with pine nuts and breadcrumb mixture. Roast a further 10 minutes or until breadcrumbs are browned.

7 Serve bake sprinkled with parsley.

prep + cook time 1 hour **serves** 4

nutritional count per serving 35.6g total fat (8.5g saturated fat); 2166kJ (517 cal); 26.3g carbohydrate; 19.2g protein; 8.2g fibre

tip If fresh borlotti beans are unavailable, replace with 1 cup drained and rinsed canned borlotti beans; there will be no need to simmer them, just add them in step 6.

free-form mushroom and cheese tart

- 60g (2 ounces) butter
- 2 tablespoons extra virgin olive oil
- 400g (12 ounces) swiss brown mushrooms, sliced thinly
- 400g (12 ounces) button mushrooms, sliced thinly
- 2 shallots (50g), chopped finely
- 200g (6½ ounces) spring onion and chive cream cheese
- 2 eggs
- ½ cup (40g) finely grated parmesan
- ¼ cup coarsely chopped fresh flat-leaf parsley
- 2 sheets puff pastry
- 1 egg, extra, beaten lightly
- 100g (3 ounces) fresh ricotta, crumbled coarsely
- 12 small fresh thyme sprigs
- ¼ cup loosely packed fresh flat-leaf parsley leaves

1 Preheat oven to 220°C/425°F. Line two oven trays with baking paper.

2 Heat half the butter and oil in a large heavy-based frying pan over high heat. Add half the mushrooms and half the shallots; season to taste; cook, stirring occasionally, 4 minutes or until golden. Transfer to a medium bowl. Repeat with remaining butter, oil, mushrooms and shallots.

3 Meanwhile, process cream cheese and eggs until smooth; stir into mushroom mixture with parmesan and chopped parsley.

4 Place a pastry sheet on each oven tray. Spread mushroom mixture evenly between sheets, into a 16cm (6½-inch) round, leaving a 4cm (1½-inch) border. Brush the border with a little of the extra egg. Fold in pastry corners, then remaining sides to partially cover filling and create a rim. Brush pastry rim with a little more egg. Scatter ricotta and thyme over filling.

5 Bake tarts 15 minutes or until pastry is puffed and golden. Serve topped with parsley leaves.

prep + cook time 1 hour **serves** 4

nutritional count per serving 69.5g total fat (37.1g saturated fat); 3877kJ (926 cal); 45g carbohydrate; 27.9g protein; 6.5g fibre

tips For the best flavour, ensure mushrooms are browned well. To achieve this, use a heavy-based frying pan and avoid moving the mushrooms around too much while they're cooking – allow them to catch and brown before turning them over. If you don't have a heavy-based pan, heat the pan first before adding the oil and butter.

If you prefer, substitute the cream cheese with garlic and herb flavoured cream cheese or soft cheese.

serving suggestion A bitter green salad.

pumpkin, capsicum and fetta stuffed mushrooms

- 350g (11 ounces) pumpkin, cut into 1cm (½-inch) cubes
- 2 tablespoons honey
- ¼ cup (60ml) olive oil
- 4 large portobello mushrooms (320g)
- 2 cloves garlic, crushed
- ¼ cup loosely packed fresh oregano leaves, chopped coarsely
- 2 teaspoons coarsely chopped fresh thyme leaves
- 180g (5½ ounces) bottled char-grilled capsicums (bell peppers), drained, sliced thinly
- 100g (3 ounces) fetta, crumbled
- ¼ cup (20g) finely grated parmesan
- 80g (2½ ounces) baby rocket (arugula) leaves
- ¼ cup (60ml) balsamic glaze
- 1 tablespoon fresh thyme leaves, extra
- 1 tablespoon fresh oregano leaves, extra

1 Preheat oven to 220°C/425°F.

2 Combine pumpkin, honey and half the oil in a large bowl; season. Transfer to a large oven tray. Roast 25 minutes or until pumpkin is tender.

3 Meanwhile, remove stalks from mushrooms. Combine garlic, herbs and remaining oil in a small bowl. Place mushrooms on a large oven tray. Spread 1 tablespoon of the herb mixture inside each mushroom cap. Season. Roast for the final 10 minutes of pumpkin cooking time.

4 Combine capsicum, fetta and roast pumpkin in a medium bowl. Spoon pumpkin mixture into mushrooms; sprinkle with parmesan. Roast mushrooms 10 minutes or until heated through and cheese is golden.

5 Serve mushrooms with rocket, drizzled with balsamic glaze. Sprinkle with extra herbs.

prep + cook time 50 minutes **serves** 4
nutritional count per serving 21.4g total fat (6.9g saturated fat); 1454kJ (347 cal); 24.8g carbohydrate; 11.2g protein; 4.9g fibre
serving suggestion Crusty bread.

leek and goat's cheese quiche

- 2 sheets puff pastry
- 10 pencil leeks (180g)
- 2 teaspoons olive oil
- 4 eggs
- 1 cup (250ml) thickened (heavy) cream
- 70g (2½ ounces) soft goat's cheese, crumbled

1 Preheat oven to 220°C/425°F.

2 Grease a 21cm x 30cm (8½-inch x 12-inch) loose-based fluted flan tin. Overlap pastry sheets slightly; press to join. Lift pastry into pan; press over base and sides, trim excess pastry. Prick base all over with a fork; place flan tin on an oven tray. Line pastry case with baking paper; fill with dried beans or rice. Bake 10 minutes. Remove paper and beans; bake a further 15 minutes or until pastry is browned and crisp.

3 Meanwhile, heat a grill plate (or grill or barbecue) to medium-high heat. Trim and wash leeks; pat dry. Brush leeks with oil; cook, turning, 7 minutes or until tender.

4 Reduce oven to 200°C/400°F.

5 Whisk eggs and cream together in a large bowl; season well. Pour egg mixture into pastry case; top with leeks and cheese.

6 Bake quiche 20 minutes or until set and golden.

prep + cook time 1 hour **serves** 4

nutritional count per serving 57.2g total fat (32.4g saturated fat); 3147kJ (752 cal); 41.3g carbohydrate; 18.7g protein; 2.4g fibre

tips Pencil leeks are also called baby or tiny leeks; use thick green onions (scallions) instead if you can't find them. This quiche will serve 8 as an entree.

serving suggestion A green salad.

sticky rice with green mango and apple salad

2 cups (400g) sticky (glutinous) rice
½ cup (25g) moist coconut flakes
2 green mangoes (660g), peeled
2 medium green-skinned apples (300g)
1 shallot (25g), sliced finely
2 fresh long red chillies, seeded, sliced thinly
4 fresh kaffir lime leaves, sliced thinly
½ cup (70g) salted peanuts, chopped coarsely
⅓ cup firmly packed fresh coriander (cilantro) leaves
⅓ cup (80ml) lime juice
½ teaspoon sesame oil
1 tablespoon rice wine vinegar
2 teaspoons finely grated palm sugar
½ teaspoon salt
1 fresh kaffir lime leaf, extra, sliced finely

1 Rinse rice in a sieve or colander under cold water until water runs clear. Place rice in a large bowl of cold water overnight.
2 Drain rice. Place rice in a muslin-lined metal or bamboo steamer; cover tightly. Place steamer over a large wok or saucepan of boiling water, making sure the bottom of the steamer does not touch the water. Steam rice, tightly covered, 35 minutes or until tender. Do not remove lid from the steamer or stir rice during cooking; check the water level occasionally, topping up with boiling water if needed.
3 Meanwhile, stir coconut in a large frying pan over high heat, stirring, until toasted lightly. Remove from pan.
4 Cut mangoes and apples into matchsticks; place in a large bowl with shallot, chilli, lime leaves, peanuts, coriander and ⅓ cup of the toasted coconut. Add combined juice, oil, vinegar, sugar and salt; toss gently to combine.
5 Serve sticky rice with salad; sprinkle with remaining coconut and extra lime leaf.

prep + cook time 40 minutes (+ standing) **serves** 4
nutritional count per serving 12.3g total fat (3g saturated fat); 2530kJ (604 cal); 106.2g carbohydrate; 12.6g protein; 6.7g fibre
tips Thai sticky rice (also known as 'glutinous' or 'sweet' rice) is a short, fat and chalky white rice that becomes soft and sticky once cooked. If you don't have time to soak the rice overnight, serve the salad with steamed jasmine rice or soaked vermicelli noodles instead.
You can use green papaya instead of the mango and apple, if you like.

wild rice and orange stuffed tomatoes

¼ cup (50g) wild rice

⅔ cup (160ml) water

4 large tomatoes (880g)

¼ cup (35g) slivered almonds

10g (½ ounce) butter

1 small brown onion (80g), chopped finely

1 tablespoon finely grated orange rind

¼ cup (60ml) orange juice

150g (4½ ounces) persian fetta

¼ cup loosely packed fresh flat-leaf parsley leaves, chopped finely

⅓ cup (95g) Greek-style yoghurt

1 tablespoon finely chopped fresh mint leaves

herb salad

120g (4 ounces) baby rocket (arugula) leaves

¾ cup loosely packed fresh flat-leaf parsley leaves

¾ cup loosely packed fresh mint leaves

1 tablespoon orange juice

1 tablespoon olive oil

1 Place rice and the water in a small saucepan over medium heat; bring to the boil. Reduce heat; simmer, covered, 30 minutes or until tender.

2 Preheat oven to 220°C/425°F.

3 Cut 1cm (½ inch) tops from tomatoes; reserve tops. Scoop out the pulp and seeds; reserve for another use. Place tomato shells in a small oiled baking dish.

4 Place nuts on an oven tray; roast in oven 5 minutes or until browned.

5 Heat butter in a large frying pan over medium heat; cook onion and rind until soft. Increase heat to high, add rice then juice; stir until liquid has evaporated. Remove from heat; stir in fetta, parsley and nuts. Season to taste. Spoon mixture into tomato shells; replace tops. Roast 10 minutes or until tomatoes are tender.

6 Meanwhile, make herb salad.

7 Combine yoghurt and mint in a small bowl.

8 Serve stuffed tomatoes with herb salad and minted yoghurt.

herb salad Place rocket and herbs in a medium bowl with combined juice and oil; toss gently to combine. Season to taste.

prep + cook time 45 minutes **serves** 4
nutritional count per serving 22.2g total fat (9g saturated fat); 1506kJ (360 cal); 21.3g carbohydrate; 14.7g protein; 7g fibre
tip You will need about 2 oranges for this recipe.

mediterranean eggplant pasta cake

- 375g (12 ounces) spaghetti
- 1 tablespoon olive oil
- 1 large brown onion (200g), chopped finely
- 2 cloves garlic, crushed
- 1½ tablespoons tomato paste
- 400g (12½ ounces) canned crushed tomatoes
- vegetable oil, for shallow-frying
- 2 medium eggplants (600g), cut lengthways into 1cm (½-inch) slices
- 1 egg
- ½ cup (40g) finely grated parmesan
- ½ cup (60g) coarsely grated cheddar
- ¼ cup loosely packed fresh basil leaves, chopped coarsely
- ¼ cup loosely packed fresh flat-leaf parsley leaves, chopped coarsely

1 Preheat oven to 200°C/400°F. Grease a deep 20cm (8-inch) round cake pan.

2 Cook spaghetti in a large saucepan of boiling salted water until just tender; drain. Place in a large heatproof bowl.

3 Heat olive oil in a large saucepan over medium heat; cook onion and garlic, stirring, 5 minutes or until onion is softened. Add paste and tomatoes; bring to the boil. Reduce heat; simmer, uncovered, 10 minutes. Season to taste.

4 Meanwhile, heat vegetable oil in a large deep frying pan; cook eggplant, in batches, until golden brown. Drain on absorbent paper.

5 Whisk egg, cheeses and herbs together with a fork in a medium bowl. Stir warm tomato sauce, then egg mixture through spaghetti; mix well.

6 Line cake pan with eggplant slices, overlapping slightly and allowing slices to hang 10cm (4 inches) over edge of pan. Pour pasta mixture into eggplant-lined pan; press mixture firmly into base and corners. Fold overhanging eggplant over filling. Cover top of pasta with remaining eggplant slices; cover pan tightly with foil.

7 Bake pasta cake 30 minutes or until heated through. Stand 10 minutes. Remove foil; invert pasta cake onto a serving plate. Cut into wedges to serve.

prep + cook time 1 hour 15 minutes (+ standing) **serves** 8
nutritional count per serving 14.1g total fat (4.1g saturated fat); 1405kJ (336 cal); 37.8g carbohydrate; 11.6g protein; 4.9g fibre
serving suggestion A green salad.

green vegetable lasagne stacks with salsa verde

4 medium zucchini (480g)

10 medium yellow patty-pan squash (300g)

375g (12 ounces) fresh lasagne sheets

200g (6½ ounces) buffalo mozzarella, sliced thinly

100g (3 ounces) rocket (arugula) leaves

cheese sauce

30g (1 ounce) butter

1½ tablespoons plain (all-purpose) flour

1 cup (250ml) milk

½ cup (60g) coarsely grated cheddar

salsa verde

⅔ cup (160ml) olive oil

2 tablespoons red wine vinegar

1 clove garlic, chopped

2 teaspoons drained baby capers, rinsed

⅔ cup loosely packed fresh coriander (cilantro) leaves

⅓ cup loosely packed fresh flat-leaf parsley leaves

1 teaspoon sea salt flakes

1 Trim zucchini and squash; slice thinly using a mandoline or V-slicer. Heat a large oiled grill plate (or grill or barbecue); cook zucchini and squash, in batches, 4 minutes each side or until browned and tender.

2 Preheat oven to 200°C/400°F.

3 Make cheese sauce, then salsa verde.

4 Cut pasta sheets into 16 x 10cm (4-inch) squares; keep pasta covered with a damp tea towel.

5 Place four pasta squares on a baking-paper-lined oven tray. Spread each square with 1 tablespoon of cheese sauce; top with half the zucchini slices. Spread another four pasta squares with 1 tablespoon each cheese sauce; place on top of zucchini. Top with squash slices. Repeat with another four pasta squares and sauce then remaining zucchini slices, pasta squares and sauce. Top with mozzarella.

6 Bake stacks 20 minutes or until cheese is lightly browned.

7 To serve, spoon 2 tablespoons salsa verde on each serving plate; position lasagne stacks in the centre, top with rocket and remaining salsa verde.

cheese sauce Melt butter in a medium saucepan over medium heat, add flour; cook, stirring, 1 minute or until mixture is very thick. Gradually add milk, stirring, until sauce boils and thickens. Remove from heat; stir in cheese. Season to taste. Cover surface tightly with plastic wrap until ready to use.

salsa verde Process ingredients until smooth.

prep + cook time 1 hour 10 minutes **serves** 4

nutritional count per serving 66.7g total fat (23.2g saturated fat); 4022kJ (960 cal); 57.5g carbohydrate; 29.5g protein; 4.5g fibre

tip It is easier to spread the sauce on the pasta squares while they are flat on a board.

kumara gnocchi with four cheese sauce

1 large kumara (orange sweet potato) (500g), chopped coarsely

2 cups (500g) plain (all-purpose) flour

1 egg, beaten lightly

50g (1½ ounces) butter

2 cups (500ml) milk

1 cup (80g) finely grated pecorino

1 cup (80g) finely grated parmesan

1 cup (120g) coarsely grated cheddar

100g (3 ounces) gorgonzola, crumbled

1 Boil, steam or microwave kumara until tender; drain well. Cool.

2 Reserve 1 tablespoon of the flour. Mash cooked kumara in a large bowl with a potato masher until smooth. Stir in remaining flour and enough egg to make a sticky dough. Knead on floured surface until mixture is smooth and just comes together.

3 Divide dough into four pieces. Working with one piece at a time, roll dough on floured surface into a 2cm (¾-inch) thick sausage shape. Using a sharp knife, cut into 2cm (¾-inch) pieces. Roll gnocchi in floured hands into a ball.

4 Roll each ball along the inside tines of a fork, pressing lightly on top of the ball with your index finger to form the gnocchi shape – grooves on one side and a dimple on the other. Place gnocchi, in single layer, on a baking-paper-lined tray. Cover with a damp tea towel; refrigerate until ready to cook.

5 Meanwhile, bring a large saucepan of salted water to the boil.

6 Melt butter in a medium saucepan over medium heat, add reserved flour; cook, stirring, 1 minute or until mixture forms a paste. Gradually add milk; stir until sauce boils and thickens. Remove from heat; stir in pecorino, parmesan and cheddar. Season to taste. Cover surface tightly with plastic wrap; keep warm.

7 Cook gnocchi in boiling water, uncovered, 3 minutes or until gnocchi float to the surface. Remove from pan with a slotted spoon; drain on absorbent paper. Add gnocchi to hot sauce, stir gently to combine.

8 Serve gnocchi topped with gorgonzola. If you like, sprinkle with fresh flat-leaf parsley and freshly ground black pepper before serving.

prep + cook time 1 hour **serves** 4

nutritional count per serving 47g total fat (29.5g saturated fat); 4545kJ (1086 cal); 114.5g carbohydrate; 47.5g protein; 7.2g fibre

rigatoni with oven-roasted vegetables

- 1 medium red onion (170g), cut into wedges
- 250g (8 ounces) yellow patty-pan squash, halved
- 12 baby zucchini (120g), halved lengthways
- ¼ cup (60ml) extra virgin olive oil
- 275g (9 ounces) baby truss roma (egg) tomatoes
- ⅓ cup (80ml) red wine
- 700g (1½ pounds) bottled tomato pasta sauce
- 500g (1 pound) rigatoni pasta
- ⅓ cup loosely packed fresh baby basil leaves

1 Preheat oven to 220°C/425°F.

2 Place onion, squash, zucchini on a large oven tray; drizzle with 2 tablespoons of the oil. Roast 20 minutes. Add tomatoes to tray, roast a further 10 minutes or until onion is golden and softened and tomatoes begin to split. Remove tomatoes from tray; cover to keep warm.

3 Heat remaining oil in a large frying pan over medium-high heat; add roasted zucchini and squash, cook, stirring, 1 minute. Add wine; cook until reduced by half. Add sauce; bring to the boil. Reduce heat to low; cook 20 minutes or until sauce is reduced slightly. Season to taste.

4 Meanwhile, cook pasta in a large saucepan of boiling salted water 8 minutes or until just tender; drain.

5 Serve pasta topped with sauce, roasted tomatoes and basil.

prep + cook time 1 hour **serves** 4

nutritional count per serving 16.3g total fat (2.6g saturated fat); 2826kJ (675 cal); 104.3g carbohydrate; 19.6g protein; 9.6g fibre

ratatouille conchiglione with butternut pumpkin sauce

2 tablespoons extra virgin olive oil

1 medium red onion (170g), chopped finely

2 cloves garlic, crushed

1 large red capsicum (bell pepper) (350g), seeded, diced into 1cm (½-inch) pieces

2 medium zucchini (240g), diced into 1cm (½-inch) pieces

1½ tablespoons tomato paste

4 medium roma (egg) tomatoes (300g), seeded, diced into 1cm (½-inch) pieces

2 tablespoons coarsely chopped oregano leaves

500g (1 pound) large conchiglione

½ cup (40g) finely grated parmesan

butternut pumpkin sauce

1½ tablespoons olive oil

1 medium brown onion (150g), chopped finely

3 cloves garlic, crushed

1kg (2 pounds) butternut pumpkin, chopped coarsely

3 cups (750ml) vegetable stock

¾ cup (180g) sour cream

1 Heat oil in a medium saucepan over medium heat; cook onion and garlic, stirring, 1 minute or until softened. Add capsicum and zucchini; cook, stirring, 5 minutes. Stir in paste and tomato; simmer, covered, 25 minutes, stirring occasionally. Stir in oregano; season to taste.

2 Meanwhile, cook pasta in a large saucepan of boiling salted water 5 minutes or until half-cooked and just beginning to soften; drain, rinse under cold water.

3 Preheat oven to 200°C/400°F.

4 Make butternut pumpkin sauce.

5 Pour pumpkin sauce into a deep 30cm x 40cm (12-inch x 16-inch), 3-litre (12-cup) large ovenproof dish. Spoon ratatouille mixture into pasta shells; place shells upright in sauce. Sprinkle with parmesan.

6 Bake pasta, covered, 25 minutes. Remove cover; bake further 10 minutes or until cheese is melted and golden. Sprinkle with extra oregano leaves.

butternut pumpkin sauce Heat oil in a large saucepan over medium heat; cook onion and garlic, stirring, 5 minutes or until golden. Add pumpkin; cook, stirring, further 5 minutes. Add stock; bring to the boil. Reduce heat; simmer, uncovered, 25 minutes or until pumpkin is tender. Add sour cream. Using hand held stick blender, blend pumpkin mixture until smooth; season to taste.

prep + cook time 1 hour 30 minutes **serves** 4

nutritional count per serving 40.1g total fat (16g saturated fat); 4018kJ (960 cal); 116.4g carbohydrate; 26.5g protein; 14.4g fibre

spinach, ricotta and pine nut cannelloni

- 100g (3 ounces) baby spinach leaves
- ½ cup (125ml) olive oil
- 1 medium brown onion (150g), chopped finely
- 1 clove garlic, crushed
- 1 tablespoon tomato paste
- ⅓ cup (80ml) white wine
- 800g (1½ pounds) canned crushed tomatoes
- 1 cup (250ml) water
- ⅓ cup (50g) pine nuts
- 800g (1½ pounds) ricotta
- 2 teaspoons finely chopped fresh lemon thyme
- 1 egg, beaten lightly
- 2 tablespoons finely grated lemon rind
- ¼ cup (60ml) lemon juice
- 16 dried cannelloni tubes (200g)
- ¾ cup (60g) grated parmesan
- 100g (3 ounces) baby rocket (arugula) leaves

1 Preheat oven to 180°C/350°F.

2 Cook spinach in a medium saucepan of boiling water 30 seconds; drain. Place cooked spinach in a medium bowl of iced water to cool. Drain; squeeze excess water from leaves. Shred spinach.

3 Heat 1 tablespoon of the oil in a medium saucepan over medium heat; cook onion and garlic, stirring, 3 minutes or until onion softens. Add paste; cook, stirring, 2 minutes. Add wine; simmer until wine is almost evaporated. Stir in tomatoes and the water; bring to the boil. Reduce heat; simmer, uncovered, 10 minutes. Season to taste.

4 Meanwhile, place pine nuts on an oven tray; roast in oven 8 minutes or until golden brown.

5 Combine cheese, spinach, pine nuts, thyme, egg, half the rind and 1 tablespoon of the juice in a medium bowl; season. Spoon mixture into a large piping bag; fill cannelloni tubes.

6 Oil a deep 20cm x 30cm (8-inch x 12-inch) ovenproof dish. Spread 1 cup of the tomato sauce over base of dish; arrange filled cannelloni tubes on sauce. Spoon remaining sauce over cannelloni; sprinkle with parmesan. Bake, covered, 30 minutes or until pasta is tender.

7 Combine remaining oil, rind and juice in a small jug; season to taste.

8 Serve cannelloni topped with rocket; drizzle with dressing.

prep + cook time 1 hour 10 minutes **serves** 4

nutritional count per serving 60.2g total fat (18.7g saturated fat); 3800kJ (908 cal); 51.7g carbohydrate; 35.3g protein; 7.3g fibre

eggplant and mushroom pasta pot pies

- 1½ tablespoons olive oil
- 1 medium brown onion (150g), chopped finely
- 2 cloves garlic, crushed
- 1 medium eggplant (300g), peeled, chopped coarsely
- 200g (6½ ounces) swiss brown mushrooms, quartered
- ⅓ cup (80ml) red wine
- 2 tablespoons tomato paste
- 800g (1½ pounds) canned crushed tomatoes
- ¼ cup loosely packed fresh basil leaves, shredded finely
- 375g (12 ounces) penne pasta
- 1 egg, beaten lightly
- ¾ cup (90g) coarsely grated cheddar
- 3 sheets puff pastry
- 1 egg white, beaten lightly

1 Preheat oven to 200°C/400°F. Oil six 2-cup (500ml) ramekins.

2 Heat oil in a large saucepan over medium-high heat; cook onion and garlic, stirring, 3 minutes or until onion is softened. Add eggplant and mushrooms; cook, stirring, 5 minutes or until mushrooms begin to colour. Add wine; cook until nearly all the liquid is evaporated. Stir in paste and tomatoes; bring to the boil. Reduce heat; simmer, uncovered, 15 minutes or until thickened. Stir in basil; season to taste.

3 Meanwhile, cook pasta in a large saucepan of boiling salted water until just tender; drain.

4 Place pasta and tomato sauce in a large heatproof bowl with combined egg and cheese; stir to combine.

5 Using one of the ramekins as a guide, cut six rounds, a little larger than the dish, from pastry.

6 Spoon pasta mixture into ramekins. Brush edges of ramekins with egg white. Top ramekins with pastry rounds, pressing gently to seal. Cut a small slit in the top of each pie. Cut remaining pastry into 1cm (½-inch) wide strips; make a lattice pattern on pastry tops, brush lightly with egg white. Place pies on an oven tray.

7 Bake pies 15 minutes or until pastry is golden brown.

prep + cook time 1 hour **makes** 6
nutritional count per pie 34.6g total fat (17.6g saturated fat); 3260kJ (778 cal); 89.5g carbohydrate; 21.7g protein; 7.8g fibre
serving suggestion A green salad

dhal-stuffed paratha with raita

60g (2 ounces) ghee (clarified butter), melted or ¼ cup (60ml) vegetable oil
1 teaspoon garam masala
2 teaspoons ground ginger
½ teaspoon ground coriander
1 clove garlic, crushed
1 long green chilli, chopped finely
1 large sprig coriander (cilantro) with root, chopped finely
400g (12½ ounces) canned brown lentils, drained, rinsed
1 cup (250ml) water
½ cup (60g) frozen peas
2½ cups (375g) atta or wholemeal plain (all-purpose) flour
¾ cup (180ml) water, approximately, extra

raita

200g (6½ ounces) Greek-style yoghurt
1 tablespoon lemon juice
2 tablespoons water
1 tablespoon finely chopped mint

1 Heat 20g (¾ ounce) of the ghee in a large saucepan over medium heat; cook spices and garlic 1 minute or until fragrant. Stir in chilli and coriander root, then lentils and the water; bring to the boil. Reduce heat; simmer, uncovered, 15 minutes or until lentils have broken down and absorbed the water.
2 Add peas to pan; cook 2 minutes or until heated through. Stir in chopped coriander leaves and stem; season to taste. Remove from heat; refrigerate until cooled.
3 Meanwhile, combine flour and 20g (¾ ounce) of the ghee in a large bowl with enough of the extra water to form a firm dough. Knead dough 5 minutes on a floured surface until smooth and elastic. Divide dough into four portions; place in a large bowl. Cover with plastic wrap.
4 Preheat oven to 120°C/250°F.
5 Roll out a portion of dough on floured surface until 5mm (¼-inch) thick. Place a quarter of the cooled dhal mixture in the centre of the round; fold dough like a parcel to enclose filling. Using a rolling pin, gently roll paratha until 5mm (¼-inch) thick, taking care not to break the dough.
6 Heat 1 teaspoon of the remaining ghee in a non-stick frying pan over medium heat; cook paratha 4 minutes each side or until golden. Transfer to an oven tray; keep warm in oven. Repeat with remaining dough, filling and ghee.
7 Meanwhile, make raita.
8 Serve paratha with raita; if you like, top with extra mint and coriander leaves.
raita Combine ingredients in a small bowl.

prep + cook time 1 hour (+ cooling & refrigeration)
serves 4
nutritional count per serving 23g total fat (13.7g saturated fat); 2600kJ (621 cal); 76.7g carbohydrate; 19.1g protein; 14.8g fibre
tip Atta is available from most major supermarkets and Indian food stores.

broccoli and cauliflower cannelloni

- 400g (12½-ounce) piece cauliflower, quartered
- 2 tablespoons olive oil
- 300g (9½ ounces) broccoli, cut into tiny florets
- 2 cloves garlic, chopped finely
- 250g (8 ounces) grape tomatoes, halved
- 1 fresh long red chilli, seeded, chopped finely
- 2 teaspoons finely chopped fresh rosemary
- 400g (12½ ounces) canned lentils, drained, rinsed
- 400g (12½ ounces) fresh ricotta
- ½ cup (40g) finely grated parmesan
- 400g (12½ ounces) canned crushed tomatoes
- 10 fresh cannelloni sheets (225g)
- ½ cup (50g) grated mozzarella

1 Preheat oven to 200°C/400°F.

2 Steam cauliflower 10 minutes or until very tender. Cool.

3 Meanwhile, heat oil in a large frying pan over medium heat; cook broccoli, garlic, grape tomatoes, chilli and rosemary, stirring, 8 minutes or until vegetables are softened. Stir in lentils; season to taste.

4 Process steamed cauliflower with ricotta and half the parmesan until smooth. Season to taste

5 Pour half of the canned tomatoes over the base of a shallow 19cm x 29cm (7¾-inch x 12-inch) ovenproof dish Place cannelloni sheets on a work surface; divide filling between sheets, spooning it lengthways across the middle. Roll up lengthways; place, seam-side down, in dish in snug rows. Spoon remaining canned tomato over the top of cannelloni, ensuring they become wet.

6 Spread cauliflower mixture over top of cannelloni, not quite spreading it to the edge of the dish. Scatter with mozzarella and remaining parmesan.

7 Bake 30 minutes or until golden and cooked through.

prep + cook time 1 hour 10 minutes **serves** 4

nutritional count per serving 26.36g total fat (10.6g saturated fat); 2382kJ (569 cal); 42.9g carbohydrate; 33.4g protein; 11.9g fibre

tip Be sure to use fresh ricotta for this recipe, available from the deli section in supermarkets and delicatessens, for the best texture and taste.

serving suggestion Mixed leaf salad.

mexican beans with cornbread and avocado salsa

- 1 tablespoon olive oil
- 1 large red onion (300g), chopped finely
- 1 medium red capsicum (bell pepper) (200g), chopped coarsely
- 1 medium green capsicum (bell pepper) (200g), chopped coarsely
- 800g (1½ pounds) canned four bean mix, drained, rinsed
- 30g (1 ounce) sachet taco spice mix
- 800g (1½ pounds) canned diced tomatoes
- 400g (12½ ounces) canned corn kernels, drained
- 1 large avocado (320g)
- ½ cup coarsely chopped coriander (cilantro)
- 1 tablespoon lime juice
- 1 long green chilli, sliced thinly

cornbread

- 1¾ cups (300g) polenta (cornmeal)
- 1 cup (120g) grated cheddar
- ½ cup (75g) self-raising flour
- 2 tablespoons finely chopped fresh chives
- 1¾ cups (430ml) buttermilk
- 2 eggs, beaten lightly
- 125g (4 ounces) butter, melted, cooled

1 Make cornbread.
2 Meanwhile, heat oil in a deep large frying pan over medium heat; cook onion and capsicums, stirring, 5 minutes or until onion is soft. Add beans and spice mix; cook, stirring, 1 minute or until fragrant.
3 Add tomatoes and corn to pan; bring to the boil. Reduce heat; simmer, uncovered, 7 minutes or until sauce thickens.
4 Coarsely chop avocado. Combine avocado, coriander, juice and half the chilli in a small bowl. Season to taste.
5 Divide bean mixture between serving plates; top with avocado salsa and remaining chilli. Serve with cornbread.
cornbread Preheat oven to 180°C/350°F. Oil a 14cm x 23cm (5½-inch x 9¼-inch) loaf pan; line base and sides with baking paper, extending the paper 5cm (2 inches) over long sides. Combine polenta, cheese, flour and chives in a large bowl. Stir in buttermilk, eggs and butter to combine (do not over-mix). Spoon mixture into pan; level surface. Bake 40 minutes. Stand in pan 5 minutes before turning, top-side up, onto a wire rack to cool.

prep + cook time 1 hour (+ cooling) **serves** 6
nutritional count per serving 40.4g total fat (19.8g saturated fat); 3432kJ (820 cal); 79g carbohydrate; 27.3g protein; 14g fibre
tip Slice any leftover cornbread and cook on a heated oiled grill plate (or grill or barbecue) until golden on both sides and heated through. Serve with poached eggs, soup or salad.

cheesy pumpkin and almond pasta bake

- 1kg (2 pounds) pumpkin, chopped coarsely
- 500g (1 pound) spiral pasta
- ½ cup (60g) ground almonds
- 2 tablespoons finely chopped fresh flat-leaf parsley
- ¼ cup finely chopped fresh chives
- ½ cup (40g) finely grated parmesan
- 1¼ cups (120g) coarsely grated cheddar
- ½ cup (40g) flaked almonds

white sauce

- 50g (1½ ounces) butter
- 2 tablespoons plain (all-purpose) flour
- 1 cup (250ml) milk
- 300ml (½ pint) pouring cream

1 Preheat oven to 160°C/325°F.

2 Boil or steam pumpkin 10 minutes or until tender. Drain; reserving 1 cup of the cooking liquid.

3 Meanwhile, cook pasta in a large saucepan of boiling salted water 8 minutes or until just tender; drain.

4 Make white sauce.

5 Place pasta and pumpkin in a large heatproof bowl with ground almonds, herbs, parmesan, 1 cup of the cheddar and reserved cooking liquid; toss to combine. Season to taste. Pour mixture into deep 3-litre (12-cup) ovenproof dish; sprinkle with remaining cheddar, then flaked almonds.

6 Bake 30 minutes or until golden brown. Serve sprinkled with a few extra parsley leaves.

white sauce Melt butter in a medium saucepan over medium heat, add flour; cook, stirring, 2 minutes or until mixture is very thick. Gradually add combined milk and cream; stir until sauce boils and thickens. Season to taste. Cover surface with plastic wrap until ready to use.

prep + cook time 50 minutes **serves** 6

nutritional count per serving 45.9g total fat (23.5g saturated fat); 3497kJ (835 cal); 76.8g carbohydrate; 25.5g protein 8.4g fibre

brown rice and pine nut stuffed vine leaves

1 cup (200g) medium-grain brown rice

1½ cups (375ml) water

½ cup (80g) pine nuts

20g (¾ ounce) butter

1 medium brown onion (150g), chopped finely

1 teaspoon ground coriander

½ cup (80g) dried currants

120g (4 ounces) labne

½ cup loosely packed fresh mint leaves, chopped finely

½ cup loosely packed fresh dill leaves, chopped finely

2 teaspoons finely grated lemon rind

2 tablespoons lemon juice

¾ cup (200g) Greek-style yoghurt

28 preserved vine leaves, approximately

1 teaspoon sumac

1 Bring rice and the water to the boil in a medium saucepan; cook, covered, over low heat 25 minutes or until tender. Remove from heat; stand, covered, 10 minutes.
2 Meanwhile, stir pine nuts in a medium frying pan over medium heat until toasted lightly. Transfer to a large bowl.
3 Heat butter in same frying pan over medium heat; cook onion and ground coriander, stirring, until browned and soft.
4 Add onion mixture and rice to large bowl with currants, labne, herbs, rind and half the juice; stir to combine. Season to taste.
5 Combine yoghurt and remaining juice in a small serving bowl; season to taste.
6 Rinse vine leaves in cold water. Drop leaves into a large saucepan of boiling water, in batches, for a few seconds, transfer to a colander; rinse under cold water, drain well. Place a vine leaf, smooth-side down, on bench; trim large stem. Place a tablespoonful of rice mixture in centre. Fold stem end and sides over filling; roll up firmly.
7 Serve rolls, drizzled with a little olive oil if you like, with yoghurt mixture sprinkled with sumac; scatter with some extra mint leaves.

prep + cook time 50 minutes **makes** 28
nutritional count per roll 4.7g total fat (1g saturated fat); 367kJ (88 cal); 9.1g carbohydrate; 1.9g protein; 1g fibre
tips Vine leaves are available from Middle Eastern food shops and some delicatessens.
If vine leaves are too small you can use two leaves together.

flatbreads with roasted peppers and zucchini

- 2 teaspoons (7g) dry yeast
- 1 teaspoon caster (superfine) sugar
- 1 cup (250ml) lukewarm water
- 2½ cups (375g) "00" flour, bread flour or plain (all-purpose) flour
- 2 teaspoons salt
- ¼ cup (60ml) extra virgin olive oil
- 2 medium brown onions (300g), sliced thinly
- 285g (9 ounces) bottled piquillo wood-roasted small whole peppers
- 2 cloves garlic, sliced thinly
- 1 medium green zucchini (120g), peeled thinly lengthways into ribbons
- 1 tablespoon fresh oregano leaves

1 Combine yeast, sugar and the water in a medium bowl of an electric mixer. Stand in a warm place 10 minutes or until bubbly.

2 Add flour, salt and 1 tablespoon of the oil to the bowl; mix with a dough hook on knead setting 8 minutes or until smooth and elastic. Cover dough; stand in a warm place 30 minutes or until doubled in size.

3 Meanwhile, heat 1 tablespoon of the oil in a large frying pan over medium heat; cook onion, stirring, 5 minutes, or until soft.

4 Preheat oven to 240°C/475°F. Oil two large oven trays.

5 Punch down dough with fist. Knead dough on a floured surface until smooth. Divide dough into four equal portions. Roll dough on floured surface into 30cm (12-inch) ovals; place on trays.

6 Drain peppers; pat dry, cut into quarters. Divide onion between bases; top with peppers, garlic and zucchini. Brush zucchini with remaining oil; season.

7 Bake flatbread 10 minutes or until bases are golden and crisp. Sprinkle with oregano; serve immediately.

prep + cook time 40 minutes (+ standing) **makes** 4

nutritional count per flatbread 15.1g total fat (2.4g saturated fat); 2125kJ (508 cal); 76g carbohydrate; 13g protein; 7.1g fibre

tips An electric mixer with a dough hook or hooks takes the hard work out of preparing the dough. If you don't have a mixer with a dough hook, knead the dough by hand on a floured surface for 10 minutes by pulling and stretching the dough at every quarter turn.

Flatbreads are best served freshly baked.

dried fig and walnut bread

- 2 teaspoons (7g) dry yeast
- 2 teaspoons caster (superfine) sugar
- 1¼ cups (310ml) lukewarm water
- 3⅓ cups (500g) "00" flour, bread flour or plain (all-purpose) flour
- 2 teaspoons sea salt flakes (10g)
- ½ cup (55g) coarsely chopped walnuts
- ¾ cup (140g) coarsely chopped dried figs

1 Combine yeast, sugar and the water in a medium bowl of an electric mixer. Stand in a warm place 10 minutes or until bubbly.
2 Add flour and salt to the bowl; mix with an electric mixer fitted with a dough hook on the knead setting 5 minutes or until smooth and elastic. Transfer dough to a board; press out to flatten slightly. Top with nuts and figs, knead into dough.
3 Place dough in an oiled bowl. Place bowl in a large plastic bag; seal bag. Stand in a warm place 45 minutes or until dough doubles in size.
4 Preheat oven to 220°C/425°F; heat an oven tray.
5 Punch down dough with fist. Knead dough on floured surface into oval shape, 28cm (11¼ inches) long. Place dough on a large piece of baking paper, then on a board. Place board in plastic bag; seal bag. Stand in a warm place 15 minutes or until risen slightly.
6 Remove bag; transfer dough to hot oven tray. Sprinkle the top with a little extra flour. Using a small sharp knife, make a shallow cut along the length of the loaf, leaving a 4cm (1½-inch) border at each end. Spray bread and tray lightly with a fine mist of water, or sprinkle lightly with water.
7 Bake bread 35 minutes or until browned and sounds hollow when tapped on the base. Transfer to wire rack to cool.

prep + cook time 1 hour (+ standing & cooling)
makes 15 slices
nutritional count per slice 3g total fat (0.2g saturated fat); 717kJ (171 cal); 30.1g carbohydrate; 4.5g protein; 2.9g fibre
tips If you don't have a mixer with a dough hook, knead the dough by hand on a lightly floured surface for 10 minutes by pulling and stretching the dough every quarter turn.
This bread is best made on the day of serving, but is also delicious toasted and served with cheese or spread with ricotta and drizzled with honey.

ciabatta dinner rolls

- 3¾ cups (560g) "00" flour, bread flour or plain (all-purpose) flour
- 3 teaspoons sea salt
- 2 teaspoons (7g) dry yeast
- 1 tablespoon extra virgin olive oil
- 2 cups (500ml) warm water
- 2 teaspoons plain (all-purpose) flour, extra

1 Place flour, salt and yeast in a large bowl of an electric mixer. Add oil and enough of the water to form a very soft, sticky dough. Mix with dough hook on knead setting 10 minutes or until smooth and elastic.

2 Lightly flour a large bowl. Scrape dough into floured bowl. Place bowl in a large plastic bag; seal bag. Stand in a warm place 1 hour or until dough doubles in size.

3 Knead dough on floured surface until smooth. Return to bowl; place in plastic bag, seal bag. Stand in a warm place 1 hour or until dough doubles in size.

4 Preheat oven to 240°C/475°F. Flour two large oven trays.

5 Divide dough into 12 pieces; shape into rounds. Place on trays. Stand 45 minutes.

6 Dust tops of rolls lightly with extra flour. Cut a slit in centre of each roll. Spray rolls lightly with a fine mist of water or sprinkle lightly with water.

7 Bake rolls 20 minutes or until lightly browned and sounds hollow when tapped on the base. For crusty rolls, spray rolls with water every 5 minutes during baking. Cool rolls on a wire rack.

prep + cook time 50 minutes (+ standing) **makes** 12
nutritional count per roll 2.1g total fat (0.3g saturated fat); 764kJ (183 cal); 34.4g carbohydrate; 5.2g protein; 1.8g fibre
tip The dough is very soft, even sloppy, and is difficult to knead by hand.
serving suggestion Serve with olive oil and balsamic vinegar.

quinoa and seed cheese damper

- ¼ cup (50g) red quinoa
- ½ cup (125ml) boiling water
- 3 cups (450g) self-raising flour
- 2 teaspoons sea salt
- 40g (1½ ounces) butter, chopped
- ¼ cup (50g) roasted buckwheat
- 2 tablespoons linseeds
- 2 tablespoons pepitas (pumpkin seed kernels)
- ¾ cup (90g) grated vintage cheddar
- ½ cup (125ml) milk
- ¾ cup (180ml) water, approximately

1 Place quinoa in a small heatproof bowl; cover with the boiling water. Stand 20 minutes. Drain well.

2 Preheat oven to 180°C/350°F. Flour a large oven tray.

3 Place flour and salt in a large bowl; rub in butter. Stir in quinoa, buckwheat, linseeds, pepitas and cheddar. Stir in milk and enough of the water to mix to a soft dough. Knead dough on a floured surface until smooth.

4 Place dough on the tray; press into a 16cm (6½-inch) round. Brush with a little extra water or milk; sprinkle with a little extra flour. Cut a 1cm (½-inch) deep cross in top of dough.

5 Bake damper 50 minutes or until golden brown and sounds hollow when tapped on the base.

prep + cook time 1 hour 5 minutes (+ standing)
makes 12 slices
nutritional count per slice 8.7g total fat (4.2g saturated fat); 1060kJ (253 cal); 34.2g carbohydrate; 8.5g protein; 2.4g fibre
tip Damper is best made on the day of serving, or reheat, wrapped in foil, in oven 15 minutes or until warmed through.
serving suggestion Butter and golden syrup or with soup.

rye, honey and seed pull-apart

- 2 cups (250g) rye flour
- 1⅓ cups (200g) "00" flour, bread flour or plain (all-purpose) flour
- 3 teaspoons sea salt
- 2 teaspoons (7g) dry yeast
- 2 tablespoons honey
- 1⅓ cups (330ml) lukewarm water
- 2 tablespoons pepitas (pumpkin seed kernels)
- 2 tablespoons sunflower seeds
- 1 tablespoon sesame seeds
- 1 tablespoon poppy seeds

1 Place flours, salt, yeast, honey and the water in a medium bowl of an electric mixer. Mix with dough hook on knead setting 10 minutes or until smooth and elastic.

2 Place dough in an oiled bowl. Place bowl in a large plastic bag; seal bag. Stand in a warm place 1 hour or until dough doubles in size.

3 Preheat oven to 200°C/400°F. Lightly flour a large oven tray.

4 Punch down dough with fist. Knead dough on lightly floured surface until smooth. Divide dough into 12 portions; knead until smooth into rounds. Combine seeds in a shallow bowl. Roll rounds in seeds to cover. Place three rounds, 1cm (½ inch) apart, in the centre of the oven tray. Position remaining nine rounds, 1cm (½ inch) apart, in a ring around the edge. Place tray in large plastic bag; seal bag. Stand in a warm place 30 minutes or until risen slightly.

5 Remove tray from plastic bag. Spray rolls and tray lightly with a fine mist of water or sprinkle lightly with water.

6 Bake rolls 20 minutes or until browned and sounds hollow when tapped on the base. Remove rolls from tray in one piece; transfer to a wire rack to cool.

prep + cook time 50 minutes (+ standing) **makes** 12
nutritional count per roll 3.2g total fat (0.6g saturated fat); 732kJ (175 cal); 30.1g carbohydrate; 4.9g protein; 3.4g fibre
tips If you don't have a mixer with a dough hook, knead the dough by hand on a lightly floured surface for 10 minutes by pulling and stretching the dough every quarter turn.
Spraying the rolls with water gives a crisp crust.
Rolls are best served slightly warm on the day of baking.

Making stock is well worth it, in terms of the quality of the finished dish. For a start, it takes little effort, and it's not rocket science; make it whenever you have some free time and feel like pottering around the kitchen, especially on a cold and dreary weekend when the stock's scent and the warmth pervade the house. Be certain to wash the vegetables well before use but forget about peeling them. While you should bring the stock to the boil initially, slowly simmering it for the duration of cooking time imbues it with the most flavour.

Vegetable stock

2 large carrots (360g), chopped coarsely

2 large parsnips (700g), chopped coarsely

4 medium onions (600g), chopped coarsely

10 sticks celery (1.5kg), trimmed, chopped coarsely

4 bay leaves

2 teaspoons black peppercorns

6 litres (24 cups) water

1 Place ingredients in a boiler; simmer, uncovered, 1½ hours.
2 Strain stock through a muslin-lined sieve or colander into a large heatproof bowl; discard solids. Allow stock to cool, cover; refrigerate until cold.

prep + cook time 1 hour 40 minutes (+ cooling & refrigeration)
makes 3.5 litres
nutritional count per 1 cup (250ml) 0.2g total fat (0g saturated fat); 151kJ (36 cal); 5.7g carbohydrate; 1.4g protein; 2.9g fibre

Pulses (dried beans, peas, lentils) have always been "poor man's meats" because they're cheap, filling and nourishing: pulses are high in the "good" carbohydrates dietary fibre, vitamins and minerals, are cholesterol-free and have little or no fat. They are also high in protein, though (except soy beans) this is incomplete protein and you need to eat a grain product such as rice, bread or corn with them to be comparable to animal protein. On the downside, pulses tend to cause flatulence but it can be minimised by pre-soaking them, then cooking well in fresh water.

Soaking pulses

Most pulses need soaking in cold water for 6–8 hours before cooking; chickpeas need up to 12 hours and broad beans up to 24. Refrigerate while soaking so they don't start to ferment. A faster way to pre-soak is to cover the pulses generously with cold, unsalted water, bring slowly to the boil, uncovered, simmer 2 minutes then remove from heat and stand, covered, for 1 hour. Soaking draws out the indigestible substances of pulses so the liquid should be drained away. Lentils don't need pre-soaking.

Cooking pulses

Cook pulses in clean, fresh water, either on the stove top or in a pressure cooker. Don't add salt to the cooking water until after the pulses are tender, as they will become tough. Soaked pulses will reduce the pressure cooking time by 5 to 10 minutes depending on the variety of pulse. Remember that pulses are dried, so they will expand during cooking; be mindful of this when deciding on quantities, and don't over-fill the saucepan or pressure cooker.

In a pressure cooker, pulses are cooked using the highest pressure, and are usually allowed to stand until the pressure releases naturally from the cooker. Always check the manual of your own cooker.

Pulses appear to store for long periods of time, but in fact are drying out; it's best to buy small quantities often and keep them in the fridge. You could also soak, rinse and drain them, then freeze in portions so they're ready to cook as needed.

Rice & other grains

Along with the usual methods, rice and other grains can be successfully cooked in a pressure cooker. As a guide, allow 3 cups water to each 1 cup of grains. Grains such as barley and brown rice are cooked using high pressure, followed by a slow release of pressure, then a quick release of pressure to stop the cooking. Short rice such as arborio, is usually cooked using high pressure, then a quick release of pressure to stop overcooking. White rice, including medium and long grain, basmati and jasmine, is cooked using high pressure, then a slow release of pressure, followed by a quick release of pressure. All grains need a little butter or oil to stop them foaming during cooking; about 1 tablespoon of either, for each cup of grain. All grains along with the water should only half-fill the pressure cooker.

Cooking times in a pressure cooker

The chart below is only a guide. For pulses, their age and moisture content will determine how long it takes until they're tender. Tasting is the best way to check. These pulses have NOT been soaked overnight. For rices and grains, these are total cooking times, including the initial time under high pressure and the slow and/or quick release of pressure times.

PULSES	
borlotti beans	30 minutes
chickpeas	45 minutes
lentils	8 minutes
red kidney beans	30 minutes
white beans	30 minutes

RICES & GRAINS	
arborio rice	6 minutes
barley	20 minutes
brown rice	20 minutes
white rice	10 minutes

glossary

artichokes
globe large flower-bud member of the thistle family; it has tough petal-like leaves, and is edible in part when cooked.
hearts tender centre of the globe artichoke; purchased, in brine, canned or in glass jars.
bamboo shoots the tender shoots of bamboo plants, available in cans; must be rinsed and drained before use.
barley a nutritious grain used in soups and stews. Hulled barley, the least processed, is high in fibre. Pearl barley has had the husk removed then been steamed and polished so that only the "pearl" of the original grain remains, much the same as white rice.
beans
borlotti also called roman beans or pink beans, can be eaten fresh or dried. Interchangeable with pinto beans due to their similarity in appearance – pale pink or beige with dark red streaks.
broad (fava) also called windsor and horse beans; available dried, fresh, canned and frozen. Fresh should be peeled twice (discarding the outer long green pod and the beige-green tough inner shell); frozen beans have had their pods removed but the beige shell still needs removal.
butter also known as lima beans; large, flat, kidney-shaped bean, off-white in colour, with a mealy texture and mild taste.
cannellini a small white bean similar in appearance and flavour to other white beans (great northern, navy or haricot), all of which can be substituted for the other. Available dried or canned.
kidney medium-sized red bean, slightly floury in texture, yet sweet in flavour.
sprouts also known as bean shoots; tender new growths of assorted beans and seeds germinated for consumption.
white a generic term we use for canned or cannellini, haricot, navy or great northern beans belonging to the same family, *phaseolus vulgaris*.
beetroot (beets) also known as red beets; firm, round root vegetable.
breadcrumbs, panko (japanese) are available in two types: larger pieces and fine crumbs. Both have a lighter texture than Western-style breadcrumbs. They are at all Asian grocery stores and, unless you make rather coarse breadcrumbs from white bread that's either quite stale or gently toasted, nothing is an adequate substitute. Has a crunchy texture with a delicate, pale golden colour.
broccolini a cross between broccoli and chinese kale; long asparagus-like stems with a long loose floret, both completely edible. Resembles broccoli but is milder and sweeter in taste.
buk choy also known as bok choy, pak choi, chinese white cabbage or chinese chard; has a fresh, mild mustard taste. Use both stems and leaves. Baby buk choy, also known as pak kat farang or shanghai bok choy, is smaller and more tender than buk choy.
butter use salted or unsalted (sweet) butter; 125g is equal to one stick of butter (4 ounces).
capers grey-green buds of a warm climate shrub (usually Mediterranean); sold dried and salted or pickled in a vinegar brine. Rinse before using.
capsicum (bell pepper) called pepper. Comes in many colours: red, green, yellow, orange and purplish-black. Be sure to discard seeds and membranes before use.
celeriac (celery root) tuberous root with knobbly brown skin, white flesh and a celery-like flavour. Keep peeled celeriac in acidulated water to stop it discolouring. It can be grated and eaten raw in salads; used in soups and stews; boiled and mashed like potatoes; or sliced thinly and deep-fried as chips.
cheese
cream cheese known as philadelphia or philly; a soft, cows'-milk cheese; sold at supermarkets. Also available as a spreadable light cream cheese – a blend of cottage and cream cheeses.
fetta Greek in origin; a crumbly textured goat- or sheep-milk cheese having a sharp, salty taste. Ripened and stored in salted whey.
fetta, persian a soft, creamy fetta marinated in a blend of olive oil, garlic, herbs and spices. It is available from most larger supermarkets.
goat's made from goat's milk, has an earthy, strong taste; available in both soft and firm textures, in various shapes and sizes, and sometimes rolled in ash or herbs.
gorgonzola a creamy blue cheese having a mild, sweet taste.
haloumi a firm, cream-coloured sheep-milk cheese matured in brine; haloumi can be grilled or fried, briefly, without breaking down. Should be eaten while still warm as it becomes tough and rubbery on cooling.
mascarpone a cultured cream product made in much the same way as yoghurt. Is whitish to creamy yellow in colour, with a soft, creamy texture and a rich, sweet, slightly acidic, taste.
mozzarella soft, spun-curd cheese; originating in southern Italy where it was traditionally made from water-buffalo milk. Now generally made from cows' milk, it is the most popular pizza cheese because of its low melting point and elasticity when heated.
parmesan also called parmigiano; is a hard, grainy cow-milk cheese originating in Italy. Reggiano is the best variety.
pecorino the Italian generic name for cheeses made from sheep's milk; hard, white to pale-yellow cheeses. If you can't find it, use parmesan.
ricotta a soft, sweet, moist, white cow-milk cheese with a low fat content and a slightly grainy texture. The name roughly translates as "cooked again" and refers to ricotta's manufacture from a whey that is itself a by-product of other cheese making.
chickpeas (garbanzo beans) also called hummus or channa; an irregularly round, sandy-coloured legume. Firm texture even after cooking, a floury mouth-feel and robust nutty flavour; available canned or dried (reconstitute for several hours in cold water before use).
chilli generally, the smaller the chilli, the hotter it is. Use rubber gloves when seeding and chopping fresh chillies as they can burn your skin. Removing seeds and membranes lessens the heat level.
long available both fresh and dried; a generic term used for any moderately hot, thin, long (6-8cm/2¼-3¼ inch) chilli.
red thai a small, hot, bright red coloured chilli.
chinese cooking wine (shao hsing) also known as chinese rice wine; made from fermented rice, wheat, sugar and salt with a 13.5% alcohol content. Inexpensive and found in Asian food shops; if you can't find it, replace with mirin or sherry.
cinnamon available in pieces (called sticks or quills) and ground into powder; one of the world's most common spices, used as a sweet, fragrant flavouring for both sweet and savoury foods.

coconut
cream obtained commercially from the first pressing of the coconut flesh alone, without the addition of water. Available in cans and cartons at most supermarkets.
desiccated concentrated, dried, unsweetened and finely shredded coconut flesh.
milk not the liquid found inside the fruit (coconut water), but the diluted liquid from the second pressing of the white flesh of a mature coconut (the first pressing produces coconut cream).
coriander (cilantro) also known as pak chee or chinese parsley; a bright-green leafy herb with a pungent flavour. Both the stems and roots of coriander are also used in cooking; wash well before using. Also available ground or as seeds; these should not be substituted for fresh coriander as the tastes are completely different.
couscous a fine, grain-like cereal product made from semolina; it swells to three or four times its original size when liquid is added.
cream
pouring also known as pure or fresh cream. It has no additives and contains a minimum fat content of 35%.
thickened (heavy) a whipping cream that contains a thickener. It has a minimum fat content of 35%.
cumin also known as zeera or comino; has a spicy, nutty flavour.
curry leaves available fresh or dried and have a mild curry flavour; use like bay leaves.
curry pastes commercially made pastes vary in strengths and flavours. Use whichever one you feel best suits your spice-level tolerance.
green the hottest of the traditional pastes; contains chilli, garlic, onion, salt, lemon grass, spices and galangal.
massaman rich, spicy flavour reminiscent of Middle Eastern cooking; favoured by southern Thai cooks for use in hot and sour stew-like curries and satay sauces.
penang based on the curries of Penang, an island off the north-west coast of Malaysia, close to the Thai border. A complex, sweet and milder variation of red curry paste; good with seafood and for adding to soups and salad dressings.
red a popular curry paste; a hot blend of red chilli, garlic, shallot, lemon grass, salt, galangal, shrimp paste, kaffir lime peel, coriander, cumin and paprika. It is milder than the hotter thai green curry paste.
edamame (shelled soy beans) available frozen from Asian food stores and some supermarkets.
eggplant also known as aubergine. Ranging in size from tiny to very large and in colour from pale green to deep purple. Can also be purchased char-grilled, packed in oil, in jars.
fennel also known as finocchio or anise; a white to very pale green-white, firm, crisp, roundish vegetable about 8-12cm in diameter. The bulb has a slightly sweet, anise flavour but the leaves have a much stronger taste. Also the name given to dried seeds having a licorice flavour.
flour
atta a fine wholemeal flour used for Indian flatbreads. It is available from most major supermarkets and Indian food stores.
plain (all-purpose) an all-purpose wheat flour.
self-raising plain flour sifted with baking powder in the proportion of 1 cup flour to 2 teaspoons baking powder.
wholemeal also known as wholewheat flour; milled with the wheat germ so is higher in fibre and more nutritional than plain flour.
gai lan also known as chinese broccoli, gai larn, kanah, gai lum and chinese kale; appreciated more for its stems than its coarse leaves.
garam masala a blend of spices that includes cardamom, cinnamon, coriander, cloves, fennel and cumin. Black pepper and chilli can be added for heat.
kaffir lime leaves also known as bai magrood. Aromatic leaves of a citrus tree; two glossy dark green leaves joined end to end, forming a rounded hourglass shape. A strip of fresh lime peel may be substituted for each kaffir lime leaf.
kecap manis a thick soy sauce with added sugar and spices. The sweetness is derived from the addition of molasses or palm sugar.
kumara (orange sweet potato) the Polynesian name of an orange-fleshed sweet potato often confused with yam.
labne is a soft cheese made by salting plain (natural) yoghurt and draining it of whey for up to 2 days until it becomes thick enough to roll into small balls, which may be scattered with or rolled in chopped herbs or spices.
lebanese cucumber short, slender and thin-skinned. Probably the most popular variety because of its tender, edible skin, tiny, yielding seeds and sweet, fresh flavoursome taste.
leek a member of the onion family, the leek resembles a green onion but is much larger and more subtle in flavour. Tender baby or pencil leeks can be eaten whole with minimal cooking but adult leeks are usually trimmed of most of the green tops then chopped or sliced.
lemon grass a tall, clumping, lemon-smelling and -tasting, sharp-edged grass; the white lower part of the stem is used, finely chopped, in cooking.
lentils (red, brown, yellow) dried pulses often identified by and named after their colour; also known as dhal.
French-style green are a local cousin to the famous (and expensive) French lentils du puy; green-blue, tiny lentils with a nutty, earthy flavour and a hardy nature that allows them to be rapidly cooked without disintegrating.
yellow also called channa dhal, are available from specialty stores and Indian food shops. They are not commonly found in supermarkets.
mushrooms
enoki clumps of long, spaghetti-like stems with tiny, snowy white caps.
flat large, flat mushrooms with a rich earthy flavour. They are sometimes misnamed field mushrooms, which are wild mushrooms.
oyster also known as abalone; grey-white mushroom shaped like a fan. Prized for their smooth texture and subtle, oyster-like flavour.
portobello are mature, fully opened swiss browns; they are larger and bigger in flavour.
shiitake when fresh are also called chinese black, forest or golden oak mushrooms; although cultivated, they are large and meaty and have the earthiness and taste of wild mushrooms. When dried, they are called donko or dried chinese mushrooms; rehydrate before use

swiss brown also known as cremini or roman mushrooms, are light brown mushrooms having a full-bodied flavour.
mustard seeds are available in black, brown or yellow varieties. They are available from major supermarkets and health-food shops.
onions
green (scallions) also known as, incorrectly, shallot; an immature onion picked before the bulb has formed. Has a long, bright-green edible stalk.
shallots also called french shallots, golden shallots or eschalots; small, brown-skinned, elongated members of the onion family.
spring have small white bulbs and long, narrow, green-leafed tops.
polenta also known as cornmeal; a flour-like cereal made of ground corn (maize). Also the name of the dish made from it.
pomegranate dark-red, leathery-skinned fresh fruit about the size of an orange filled with hundreds of seeds, each wrapped in an edible lucent-crimson pulp having a unique tangy sweet-sour flavour.
pomegranate molasses not to be confused with pomegranate syrup or grenadine (used in cocktails); pomegranate molasses is thicker, browner and more concentrated in flavour – tart, sharp, slightly sweet and fruity. Buy from Middle Eastern food stores or specialty food shops
preserved lemon rind a North African specialty; lemons are quartered and preserved in salt and lemon juice or water. To use, remove and discard pulp, squeeze juice from rind, rinse rind well; slice thinly. Once opened, store under refrigeration.
quinoa pronounced keen-wa; is a gluten-free grain. It has a delicate, slightly nutty taste and chewy texture.
radicchio a red-leafed Italian chicory with a refreshing bitter taste that's eaten raw and grilled. Comes in varieties named after their places of origin, such as round-headed Verona or long-headed Treviso.
ras el hanout a classic spice blend used in Moroccan cooking. The name means 'top of the shop' and is the very best spice blend a spice merchant has to offer. Most versions contain over a dozen spices, including cardamom, nutmeg, mace, cinnamon and ground chilli.
rice
arborio small, round grain rice well-suited to absorb a large amount of liquid; the high level of starch makes it especially suitable for risottos for its classic creaminess.
basmati a white, fragrant long-grained rice. Wash several times before cooking.
jasmine fragrant long-grained rice; white rice can be substituted, but will not taste the same.
wild not a member of the rice family but the seed of an aquatic grass native to the cold regions of North America. Wild rice has a strong nutty taste and can be expensive, so is best combined with other rices.
risoni small rice-shape pasta; very similar to another small pasta, orzo.
saffron available ground or in strands; imparts a yellow-orange colour to food once infused. The quality can vary greatly; the best is the most expensive spice in the world.
sambal oelek (also ulek or olek) Indonesian in origin; a salty paste made from ground chillies and vinegar. Found in supermarkets and Asian food stores.
silver beet also known as swiss chard; mistakenly called spinach.
snow peas also called mange tout (eat all). Snow pea tendrils, the growing shoots of the plant, are also available at greengrocers. Snow pea sprouts are the tender new growths of snow peas.
soy sauce made from fermented soya beans. Several variations are available in most supermarkets and Asian food stores. We use japanese soy sauce unless otherwise indicated.
spinach also known as english spinach and, incorrectly, silver beet.
split peas a variety of yellow or green pea grown specifically for drying. When dried, the peas usually split along a natural seam. Whole and split dried peas are available packaged in supermarkets and in bulk in health-food stores.
sugar, brown very soft, finely granulated sugar retaining molasses for its characteristic colour and flavour.
sumac a purple-red, astringent spice ground from berries growing on shrubs that flourish wild around the mediterranean; adds a tart, lemony flavour to food. Available from spice shops and major supermarkets.
tahini a rich, sesame-seed paste, used in most Middle-Eastern cuisines, especially Lebanese, in dips and sauces.
tomato
bottled pasta sauce a prepared sauce; a blend of tomatoes, herbs and spices.
canned whole peeled tomatoes in natural juices; available crushed, chopped or diced. Use undrained.
paste triple-concentrated tomato puree used to flavour soups, stews and sauces.
puree canned pureed tomatoes (not tomato paste).
truss small vine-ripened tomatoes with vine still attached.
vinegar
balsamic originally from Modena, Italy, there are now many balsamic vinegars on the market ranging in pungency and quality depending on how, and for how long, they have been aged. Quality can be determined up to a point by price; use the most expensive sparingly.
white made from spirit of cane sugar.
water chestnut resembles a chestnut in appearance, hence the English name. They are small brown tubers with a crisp, white, nutty-tasting flesh. Their crunchy texture is best experienced fresh, however, canned water chestnuts are more easily obtained.
watercress one of the cress family, a large group of peppery greens. Highly perishable, so must be used as soon as possible after purchase.
wombok (napa cabbage) also known as peking cabbage, chinese cabbage or petsai; elongated in shape with pale green, crinkly leaves.
yeast (dried and fresh), a raising agent used in dough making. Granular (7g sachets) and fresh compressed (20g blocks) yeast can almost always be substituted for the other.
yoghurt, Greek-style plain yoghurt strained in a cloth (traditionally muslin) to remove the whey and to give it a creamy consistency.
za'atar a Middle Eastern herb and spice mixture which varies; always includes thyme, with ground sumac and, usually, toasted sesame seeds.
zucchini also called courgette; small, pale- or dark-green or yellow vegetable of the squash family. Harvested when young, its edible flowers can be stuffed and deep-fried.

conversion chart

measures

One Australian metric measuring cup holds approximately 250ml; one Australian metric tablespoon holds 20ml; one Australian metric teaspoon holds 5ml.
The difference between one country's measuring cups and another's is within a two- or three-teaspoon variance, and will not affect your cooking results.
North America, New Zealand and the United Kingdom use a 15ml tablespoon.
All cup and spoon measurements are level. The most accurate way of measuring dry ingredients is to weigh them. When measuring liquids, use a clear glass or plastic jug with the metric markings.
The imperial measurements used in these recipes are approximate only. Measurements for cake pans are approximate only. Using same-shaped cake pans of a similar size should not affect the outcome of your baking. We measure the inside top of the cake pan to determine sizes.
We use large eggs with an average weight of 60g.

dry measures

metric	imperial
15g	½oz
30g	1oz
60g	2oz
90g	3oz
125g	4oz (¼lb)
155g	5oz
185g	6oz
220g	7oz
250g	8oz (½lb)
280g	9oz
315g	10oz
345g	11oz
375g	12oz (¾lb)
410g	13oz
440g	14oz
470g	15oz
500g	16oz (1lb)
750g	24oz (1½lb)
1kg	32oz (2lb)

liquid measures

metric	imperial
30ml	1 fluid oz
60ml	2 fluid oz
100ml	3 fluid oz
125ml	4 fluid oz
150ml	5 fluid oz
190ml	6 fluid oz
250ml	8 fluid oz
300ml	10 fluid oz
500ml	16 fluid oz
600ml	20 fluid oz
1000ml (1 litre)	1¾ pints

length measures

metric	imperial
3mm	⅛in
6mm	¼in
1cm	½in
2cm	¾in
2.5cm	1in
5cm	2in
6cm	2½in
8cm	3in
10cm	4in
13cm	5in
15cm	6in
18cm	7in
20cm	8in
22cm	9in
25cm	10in
28cm	11in
30cm	12in (1ft)

oven temperatures

The oven temperatures in this book are for conventional ovens; if you have a fan-forced oven, decrease the temperature by 10-20 degrees.

	°C (CELSIUS)	°F (FAHRENHEIT)
Very slow	120	250
Slow	150	300
Moderately slow	160	325
Moderate	180	350
Moderately hot	200	400
Hot	220	425
Very hot	240	475

index

A

artichokes and garlic, roasted, fettuccine with burnt sage butter 155
artichokes, mushy fresh peas with almonds and 76
asparagus, roasted, and smashed potatoes 87

B

barley and haloumi, roasted broccoli with 118
barley and vegetable soup with crunchy seeds 41
barley salad, green 118
barley with pistachio and green olives 123
bean and leek risoni 148
bean stew, italian 133
beans, mexican, with cornbread and avocado salsa 216
beetroot, baby, green lentil, watercress and hazelnut salad 57
beetroot, roasted, with goat's cheese and walnuts 91
bread, dried fig and walnut 224
broad bean and chickpea soup, spiced, with eggs and cumin salt 30
broccoli and cauliflower cannelloni 215
broccoli, roasted, with barley and haloumi 118
brown fried rice with carrot, cabbage and red onion 123
brown rice and pine nut stuffed vine leaves 220
brussels sprout salad with poached egg 58

C

capsicum sauce, creamy spiced roast, farfalle with 144
caramelised onion and fennel soup with twice-baked cheese soufflés 180
carrot soup, spiced, with smoked almonds 16
carrots, moroccan, with chickpeas and spinach couscous 144
cauliflower and chickpea curry 166
cauliflower and rocket risotto 124
chickpea(s)
- moroccan pumpkin and chickpea salad 68

(*chickpea(s)* continued)
- moroccan carrots with chickpeas and spinach couscous 144
- smoky chickpea stew 126
- spiced chickpea and broad bean soup with eggs and cumin salt 30
- tomato, mozzarella and chickpea pan bake 104
- za'atar spiced chickpea salad with fetta and mint 129

ciabatta dinner rolls 227
corn and kidney bean quesadillas with tomato salsa 75
corn soup with parmesan crisps and chilli 21
cornbread 216
couscous
- couscous, red cabbage and walnut salad 143
- jewelled couscous salad 46
- moroccan carrots with chickpeas and spinach couscous 144
- with spiced eggplant and lemony yoghurt 156

curry
- breakfast 169
- cauliflower and chickpea 166
- japanese pumpkin 170
- potato and egg rendang 173
- red tofu 173
- thai eggplant 166

D

damper, quinoa and seed cheese 228
dhal, yellow, with spinach 165
dhal-stuffed paratha with raita 212
dressing 67, 87, 143
- cashew yoghurt 130
- curry dressing 83
- hazelnut dressing 92
- hummus dressing 79
- red wine vinegar dressing 91
- sesame dressing 63

dried fig and walnut bread 224

E

egg salad, new curried 107
egg, spinach and tomato bread cases, individual 103
eggplant and mushroom pasta pot pies 211
eggplant curry, thai 166
eggplant pasta cake, mediterranean 199
eggplant, baked, greek 184
eggplant, spiced, and lemony yoghurt, couscous with 156
eggs, turkish 99

F

farfalle with creamy spiced roast capsicum sauce 144
fattoush 60
fennel and potatoes, roasted baby parsnips 87
fennel and tomato soup with rouille 33
fettuccine with burnt sage butter, roasted artichokes and garlic 155
fig, dried, and walnut bread 224
flatbreads with roasted peppers and zucchini 223
flatbreads with spinach, lentil and zucchini salad 130
free-form mushroom and cheese tart 188
fried rice, brown, with carrot, cabbage and red onion 123

G

gnocchi, kumara, with four cheese sauce 203
goat's cheese and walnuts, roasted beetroot with 91
goat's cheese soufflés, potato, spinach and 108
goat's cheese, and watercress, ravioli 160
goat's cheese, leek and, quiche 192
grape and apple salad with goat's cheese 50
greek baked eggplant 184
green barley salad 118
green vegetable lasagne stacks with salsa verde 200

H

haloumi, seared, with zucchini and basil 100

K

kidney bean, and corn, quesadillas with tomato salsa 75

kidney beans with eggs and coriander 133
kumara and lentil soup, curried 29
kumara gnocchi with four
cheese sauce 203
kumara rösti with portobello
mushrooms 84

L

labne, tomato salad with 64
laksa, vegetable, with fried tofu 37
lasagne stacks, green vegetable,
with salsa verde 200
leek and goat's cheese quiche 192
lentil soup, curried kumara and 29
lentil, gorgonzola and witlof salad 54
lima bean soup, greek, with fetta
and olives 18
linguine primavera and poached eggs 139
linguine with squash, baby brussels
sprouts and spring onions 151

M

melon, cucumber and white onion
salad 67
mexican beans with cornbread and
avocado salsa 216
mexican stuffed potatoes with spiced
tomato and avocado salsa 88
moroccan carrots with chickpeas and
spinach couscous 144
moroccan pumpkin and chickpea salad 68
mung bean, crunchy, and coriander
salad 53
mushroom
and water chestnut steamed
wontons 183
egg and mushroom pasta pot pies 211
free-form mushroom and
cheese tart 188
mushroom soup with herbed goat's
cheese croûtes 22
pumpkin, capsicum and fetta
stuffed mushrooms 191
soft polenta with mixed
mushrooms 120
spaghetti with mushrooms and
breadcrumbs 140
mushy fresh peas with almonds and
artichokes 76

O

omelette rolls, vegetable curry 176
omelette, asian-style, with
glass noodles 111

P

pancakes, ricotta and basil, with
tomato and rocket salad 96
paratha, dhal-stuffed, with raita 212
parsnips, baby, fennel and potatoes,
roasted 87
pasta
bean and leek risoni 148
broccoli and cauliflower cannelloni 215
cheesy pumpkin and almond
pasta bake 219
eggplant and mushroom pasta
pot pies 211
farfalle with creamy spiced roast
capsicum sauce 144
fettuccine with burnt sage butter,
roasted artichokes and garlic 155
green vegetable lasagne stacks
with salsa verde 200
kumara gnocchi with four
cheese sauce 203
linguine primavera and poached
eggs 139
linguine with squash, baby brussels
sprouts and spring onions 151
mediterranean eggplant pasta cake 199
ratatouille conchiglione with
butternut pumpkin sauce 207
rigatoni with oven-roasted
vegetables 204
spaghetti with mushrooms and
breadcrumbs 140
spaghetti with radicchio, pear,
blue cheese and walnuts 159
spinach, ricotta and pine nut
cannelloni 208
watercress and goat's cheese ravioli 160
wholemeal spaghetti with green lentils,
mushrooms and parsley butter 152
zesty rocket and lemon pesto
spaghetti 140
peas, mushy fresh, with almonds
and artichokes 76
pies, vegie curry 175
pistachio and green olives, barley with 123
polenta, soft, with mixed mushrooms 120
portobello bruschetta with grilled
capsicum sauce 80
potato and egg rendang 173
potato, saffron, soup with capsicum
and almonds 18
potato, spinach and goat's cheese
soufflés 108
potatoes, mexican stuffed, with spiced
tomato and avocado salsa 88
primavera soup with pangrattato 25
pumpkin
cheesy pumpkin and almond
pasta bake 219
japanese pumpkin curry 170
moroccan pumpkin and
chickpea salad 68
pumpkin and ricotta bake 187
pumpkin, capsicum and fetta
stuffed mushrooms 191
roast cumin pumpkin and parsnip
with hummus dressing 79

Q

quesadillas, corn and kidney bean,
with tomato salsa 75
quiche, leek and goat's cheese 192
quinoa and seed cheese damper 228
quinoa, zucchini and fetta salad 117

R

radicchio and pear risotto 114
ratatouille conchiglione with butternut
pumpkin sauce 207
ratatouille soup with pistou 34
ravioli, watercress and goat's cheese 160
red beans and rice, spicy 134
red salad 58
red tofu curry 173
rice
brown fried rice with carrot, cabbage
and red onion 123
cauliflower and rocket risotto 124
crunchy Asian rice salad 63
radicchio and pear risotto 114
sticky rice with green mango and
apple salad 195
wild rice and orange stuffed
tomatoes 196

ricotta and basil pancakes with
tomato and rocket salad 96
ricotta, pumpkin and, bake 187
rigatoni with oven-roasted vegetables 204
risotto, cauliflower and rocket 124
risotto, radicchio and pear 114
rösti, kumara, with portobello
mushrooms 84
ruby grapefruit, orange and basil salad 50
rye, honey and seed pull-apart 231

S

saffron potato soup with capsicum
and almonds 18
salad
baby beetroot, green lentil, watercress
and hazelnut salad 57
baby rocket, strawberry and
walnut salad 67
brussels sprout salad with
poached egg 58
couscous, red cabbage and walnut 143
crunchy Asian rice salad 63
crunchy mung bean and coriander 53
fattoush 60
grape and apple salad with
goat's cheese 50
green barley 118
greenest green 49
jewelled couscous 46
lentil, gorgonzola and witlof 54
melon, cucumber and white onion 67
moroccan pumpkin and chickpea 68
new curried egg 107
quinoa, zucchini and fetta 117
red salad 58
ruby grapefruit, orange and basil 50
sticky rice with green mango
and apple 195
tomato salad with labne and za'atar 64
warm green salad with soft eggs
and hazelnut dressing 92
za'atar spiced chickpea salad
with fetta and mint 129
sesame and peanut soba noodles 148
silver beet, ricotta and porcini
fillo stacks 72
soufflés, potato, spinach and goat's
cheese 108
soufflés, twice-baked cheese, caramelised
onion and fennel soup with 180
soup
barley and vegetable soup with
crunchy seeds 41
(*soup* continued)
caramelised onion and fennel soup
with twice-baked cheese soufflés 180
chinese noodle, tofu and vegetable 26
corn soup with parmesan
crisps and chilli 21
curried kumara and lentil soup 29
fennel and tomato soup with rouille 33
greek lima bean soup with fetta
and olives 18
mushroom soup with herbed goat's
cheese croûtes 22
primavera soup with pangrattato 25
ratatouille soup with pistou 34
saffron potato soup with capsicum
and almonds 18
spiced carrot soup with smoked
almonds 16
spiced chickpea and broad bean soup
with eggs and cumin salt 30
spinach, rocket and pea soup
with brie croûtes 42
tom yum soup 38
vegetable laksa with fried tofu 37
spaghetti with mushrooms and
breadcrumbs 140
spaghetti with radicchio, pear, blue
cheese and walnuts 159
spaghetti, wholemeal, with green lentils,
mushrooms and parsley butter 152
spiced carrot soup with smoked
almonds 16
spiced chickpea and broad bean soup
with eggs and cumin salt 30
spiced tomato and avocado salsa,
mexican stuffed potatoes with 88
spicy red beans and rice 134
spinach, lentil and zucchini salad,
flatbreads with 130
spinach, ricotta and pine nut cannelloni
208
spinach, rocket and pea soup with
brie croûtes 42
squash, baby brussels sprouts and
spring onions, linguine with 151
steamed vegetables with curry
dressing 83
sticky rice with green mango and
apple salad 195

T

tart, free-form mushroom and cheese 188
tarts, zucchini 99
thai eggplant curry 166
tofu
chinese noodle, tofu and
vegetable soup 26
red tofu curry 173
vegetable laksa with fried tofu 37
tom yum soup 38
tomato salad with labne and za'atar 64
tomato, mozzarella and chickpea
pan bake 104
tomatoes, stuffed, wild rice and
orange 196
turkish eggs 99

V

vegetable curry omelette rolls 176
vegetable laksa with fried tofu 37
vegetable stock 232
vegetable, and barley, soup with
crunchy seeds 41
vegetables, steamed, with curry
dressing 83
vegie curry pies 175
vine leaves, stuffed, brown rice and
pine nut 220

W

warm green salad with soft eggs and
hazelnut dressing 92
watercress and goat's cheese ravioli 160
wholemeal spaghetti with green lentils,
mushrooms and parsley butter 152
wild rice and orange stuffed tomatoes 196
wontons, steamed, mushrooms and
water chestnut 183

Z

za'atar spiced chickpea salad with
fetta and mint 129
zesty rocket and lemon pesto spaghetti
140
zucchini
flatbreads with roasted peppers
and zucchini 223
quinoa zucchini and fetta salad 117
seared haloumi with zucchini
and basil 100
zucchini tarts 99